# AFTER

## THE

# RAIN

# AFTER

### THE

Gentle Reminders
for Healing, Courage,
and Self-Love

AIN

ALEXANDRA ELLE

CHRONICLE BOOKS
SAN FRANCISCO

Library of Congress Cataloging-in-Publication Data available.

ISBN 978-1-7972-0010-1

Manufactured in China.

Design by Vanessa Dina.

Names printed with an asterisk have been changed.

10 9 8 7 6 5 4 3 2

Chronicle books and gifts are available at special quantity discounts to corporations, professional associations, literacy programs, and other organizations. For details and discount information, please contact our premiums department at corporatesales@chroniclebooks.com or at 1-800-759-0190.

Chronicle Books LLC
680 Second Street
San Francisco, California 94107
www.chroniclebooks.com

To everyone learning how to dance in the rain.

Your storms do not define you.

Trust your pilgrimage and uncover your joy.

You are worthy.

Finding peace in the storms that show up in my life is a lesson that I continue to work through on a daily basis. It's mucky, uncomfortable, and at times feels impossible to stand in. Even after all the years I've been doing this work and all the progress I've made to grasp and hold on to self-love, the roaring thunder of emotions can sometimes still have the power to drown out any ounce of clarity that could possibly make sense or make me feel at ease. When I'm trekking through the middle of turbulence, it is difficult to envision the beauty, or blessings, after the storm.

The greatest lesson my healing and self-awareness have taught me is this: Despite all the work I have done to arrive in a place of joy and contentment, there is still so much more to be considered. There is still much more to be done. Unfolding never stops, no matter how successful we become, how full we feel, or how at ease we may believe ourselves to be. There is always a next step, another way, and more to absorb. Growing up, I thought my childhood would last forever, and then I'd step into adulthood, knowing everything I know now with little to no experience, and thrive! That is not how life happened for me, or anyone else I know. I wish someone told my younger self that there is no end point or arrival date, ever. If I were speaking to thirteen-year-old me today, I would tell her that when we stop learning how to move through adversity, if we choose to sit in our enlightenment without exploring further evolution, we become stagnant and satisfied with stunted growth. The goal for me is to continue learning how to dance in the rain, even if it's mixed with tears as I learn my way. All of life's complexities are showing me that my intention should always be rooted in addressing the storms, instead of hiding from them. As I mature, shift, and take shape, I am finding new ways to navigate the valleys of suffering that are predestined to occur.

During my crusade through self-discovery, I am continuously reminded that I am a student, and I will always be one. That is the gift even when we feel uncertain or lost in our current season. In order to grow, we, like the transition of autumn and rebirth of spring, must also prepare to shed and begin again. In pursuance of blooming, there must be rain. As we wait for the downpour to cease and new light to emerge, patience is our best and dearest friend. The sun will be on the horizon again, eventually. I am learning on a daily basis how to lead and live a meaningful life. How to create space for my healing and grief to coexist, paint my own picture, tell my own story, and remove the shame that comes with emotional duality. Often, it isn't until we are flooded with gratitude from our vast and unique experiences, even the ones that hurt the most, that we are given the gift of glory.

This book is a collection of lessons, reminders, and meditations that have helped push me into a place of self-compassion and reflection. Through these lessons, I have discovered grace and awareness of possibility. My writing is birthed from a place of resilience, perseverance, and the discovery of self-advocacy. It's rooted in the soil of finding my footing, reveling in belonging, and owning my truth in a way that is honest and faithful to the girl I was and the woman I am today. After the rain, truth finds a way to shine through the clouds, reminding us all that we are deserving of healing. That we're worthy of change. That we are built to expand and stretch into our best selves.

As you travel your own path, no matter the season or situation, I want this body of work to give you hope. Envelop yourself in these pages for comfort, belonging, and a sense of comradery. I hope these words settle into the soft part of your heart with this simple reminder: You are not alone. Here's to dancing in the rain, and believing that triumph is on the other side of trepidation.

Yours truly,
**ALEX ELLE**

I am my own.
I am enough.
I am rooted in love.

My life is abundant.
My heart is resilient.
My happiness is important.

Nothing has the power to break
or destroy me. I am
whole even through hurt.

# LIFE
## LES

SONS

# Change

When I think of change, I like to imagine the transitions between seasons. This helps me view change as a beautiful unfolding, rather than a terrifying process. I've always been fascinated with autumn foliage; I'm amazed by how the leaves wither and wilt before falling away. I often wonder what gave perennial plants and trees enough trust in their Creator to be born again come spring. I like to think their fiery golden hues represent the bravery it takes to shed what is no longer needed, without question or doubt.

Letting go has never been my strength. If I were a tree, I'd be scared out of my mind that my leaves would never return. But in my ideal world, change wouldn't incite fear. Instead, it would encourage shedding as part of the natural process of becoming whole and lush.

The shifting I've grown to know over the years isn't appealing, dreamy, or intrepidly anticipated. Instead, it's unsettling, at times

chaotic, and often terrifying. Learning how
to lean into change and not run from it
has been a pain in the ass on almost all
occasions in my life. My relationship with
necessary adjusting has been both tumultu-
ous and invigorating. Through the inevitable
discomfort of having to unlearn old bad
habits, I had to take ownership of redefining
my sense of self so that I could discover my
purpose. And that meant embracing time
alone, a season of complete solitude. Trans-
forming on my own wasn't my first choice,
but it's grown to be my most treasured.
Being alone showed me that I could shed,
release, and outgrow anything, including my
old ways and bad habits, that didn't serve me
well. Change taught me the importance of
self-autonomy, which I never quite believed I
would come to know.

The notion that I had the power to outgrow
who I was, and start a new relationship
with who I wanted to be, became clear to
me when I was about twenty-one. Even
though it felt impossible, I wanted badly
to reroute my life and find joy, but I didn't
know where to start. Searching for and
finding my *how* was the scariest thing I'd
done in my life. Changing meant I had to
start with being honest about who I was and
who I wanted to be. It meant learning the

difference between being alone and being lonely. I had to get my stuff together. And in order to do that, I knew I needed to leave people behind who were distracting me from my growth. I had to start from scratch and acknowledge my roles in the cycles that I said I wanted to break. Committing to change meant challenges and trust, which stripped me of everything that I knew.

It was the summer of 2011, and I was approaching my twenty-second birthday. The DC metro area was oppressive and brutally hot. I'd just been fired from my first real job as an officer manager, where I was making eighteen dollars an hour. I thought that I was rolling in dough. The gig was sweet and easy, but I wasn't a good employee. In fact, leading up to that job, I had been a historically terrible staff member at every single place I'd been employed, from a retail job at Forever 21 for a day to nannying. I often joke that I am likely still used as an example of what not to be and do at staff meetings. I did not like working for anyone—families, corporations, or nonprofits. My attitude made that clear to my employers. I was miserable at work because I had no idea what I wanted to do or be in life, and that cluelessness made things stressful. I was overwhelmed with the pressure of having to figure it out. Having a boss and reporting to someone, punching a time card, and needing to be someplace that sucked the life out of me wasn't my first choice. It actually wasn't a choice at all. When I was seven I looked at my nana and said, "When I grow up, I want to work for myself so I can be with my family." Even as a child, I knew what I wanted my life to be, and it wasn't rooted in being an unhappy employee. But now as an adult with a child, I had to do what I had to do for her well-being, no matter how unfulfilling.

I worked at that sweet gig for only three months. It was short lived because apparently I was the worst office manager to ever grace the front desk of that small organization. They took a chance on a young black single mother who had an outstanding resume filled with jobs I hated. My mom worked in HR at the time and had hooked up my resume in all the right ways. I remember I showed up to the interview in a black pinstripe pantsuit from H&M, a baby-blue satin button-up shirt, and kitten heels. I felt like I was performing for a role on *The Office*. On paper, I was amazing; in reality, they were absolutely right to fire me.

On the first day, I looked the part, but I was awful at the job and I wasn't managing a damn thing but selfies in the bathroom mirror. The office could've caught on fire and I likely wouldn't have been there in time to catch it. My maturity level wasn't at its peak yet. Or, perhaps, I was too miserable to see past the fact that I had a job to do. One that was actually considered important. Working at a job I didn't want was the reason behind my unprofessionalism and foolishness. I found out I was being let go through an email sent to the entire staff. Whoever sent it forgot to remove me from the thread. It was an embarrassing relief that was bound to happen. Someone way more committed than me deserved that job and the decent pay. The message read as follows:

*All,*

*Who is going to fire her? We need to let Alex go before the end of the week. I called our former office manager to see if there was any way she could please come back, she said yes :o). The director gave us the go-ahead to increase her pay, too. She can start as soon as Friday. The new girl is just not working out.*

*Any takers?*

*—Bonnie\**

One of my former coworkers was nice enough to offer to help coach me. She was the only other black lady in the organization, so I know she was trying to look out for me, despite the fact that I didn't deserve it.

*Bonnie,*

*Do we really need to fire her? Maybe I can help her get better? She's young and new and likely just needs a little molding. I am willing to help if there's any chance of flexibility.*

*—Sharon\**

The answer to that was a clear and hard no.

*Sharon,*

*Mae\* is starting this Friday. Alex has to go, unfortunately. Are you open to letting her know tomorrow morning? Oh, and can you pack up her belongings so they'll be ready when she comes in?*

*Thanks,*

*B.*

I decided to chime in since no one seemed to notice that I was on the thread.

*Wait, what? I'm fired?*

*—Alex*
  *Office Manager*

Sharon called me shortly after with the news I already knew. "I'm sorry you had to find out this way, Alex," was the first thing out of her mouth. I was out the door the next day, my belongings waiting for me in a small brown lunch bag on the desk, folded neatly and sealed with a yellow paper clip. Mae was just leaving upon my arrival. She looked right past me and at the floor. Everyone was uneasy that morning during my ten-minute visit. I wouldn't be surprised if they cheered when they saw my car leave the parking lot. I look back and laugh now, but yes, I was that bad at being an office manager.

I needed to find another job, again. One where I couldn't completely fail, where I could write poetry during downtime, and that was located close enough to a USPS that I could drop off my jewelry orders during lunch. Essentially, I needed a position that didn't require managing an office or

**20**

interacting with customers all day. I wasn't good at office work, retail, or waitressing. I wanted to nurture my creative heart and work for myself, like seven-year-old me told her nana. My end goal was to make a living doing things I loved, but there was seemingly no way I could achieve that while being a dropout journalism student who made jewelry on the side to make ends meet, while also trying to get a self-published book off the ground. It all felt impossible and unrealistic. Not to mention that my parents were not supportive. "You want to do what?" my mom would ask. "What about your child? You're not going to have health insurance. How are you going to save money? Writers don't make anything. Your jewelry making isn't sustainable. Entrepreneurship is hard; you're *going* to struggle. This is selfish to even think about. Why would you do this?" My stepdad is a man of few words, but I am pretty sure they were in agreement.

While those concerns were valid and pessimism was to be expected, I tried to see where they were coming from. My mom made some good points—great points, actually. And I was well aware that people, including myself, fear the unknown. It always feels much easier to play it safe. It makes more sense to stick with a guarantee than risk everything and disappoint. But I was ready for something more. *More* meant changing my ways, finding a respectable work ethic, saving my money, and doing things differently. I thought about every question my mom asked me. I weighed the pros and cons. I used the doubt she had, and the self-doubt I'd grown accustomed to, as fuel to make a new path for myself. If I didn't believe in myself, who would?

So I started there. I made the choice to set myself up for abundance and joy. It was time to get my life together. And while sometimes I felt like I was making slow and steady progress, the rate I was going wasn't sufficient. It was lazy, even. I wasn't trying my best, and it was time to get out of my own my way. I felt like a robot trapped in a cycle of never-ending mediocrity. I'd gotten comfortable with being average. For me, change required being brave enough to let go and vulnerable enough to start over, even if that meant trying more than once or twice to get it right.

The last job I would ever have shaped me into who I am today in my career. I found the listing as I scoured job postings for a position that I could succeed in and that

I would semi-enjoy. I wanted to be at a place that was doing good in the world, or at least trying to, despite it not being my forever job. The program coordinator/ administrative assistant position at a small organization in Northwest DC caught my eye. I interviewed with a man who would, eight months later, push me out the door into my passion and remind me of why change had to take precedence in my life.

I will never forget my last day at the office. My supervisor, Sam*, was in a particularly bad mood. He'd always been temperamental, but that day he was exceptionally so. I was helping a few team members with a staff project when Sam barged in to the room telling me how I needed to order more coffee filters for the kitchen, immediately. I let him know that the order had been placed earlier that morning and the filters were scheduled to arrive in a few days.

"Why are you back here, anyway?" Sam asked with an irritated tone of voice. "You belong up front at your desk."

I explained that I was helping my coworkers decorate one of our colleagues' desks before her last day in the office. Remnants of colorful construction and tissue paper were spread around us. I tried to keep my composure in the midst of feeling berated and insulted.

"Cute. But you need to go back to your desk. This little project isn't in your job description; waiting for UPS boxes is, though," Sam said sarcastically.

As he turned to walk out the door, I heard him say under his breath, "Don't forget your place here."

"Excuse me?" I said.

Sam scoffed and answered, "You're a low-budget employee; we don't *need* people like you. You should take note of that. No offense, of course, but you are. Let's not forget the chain of command, okay?"

The curtness in his voice was infuriating. Sam was known around the office for being difficult and irrational, but this attack seemed like he was waiting to project his misery onto someone. I tried my best to remember the compassionate character trait I was working on, but it took all of me not to cuss him out, even though I knew I didn't want to stoop to his level.

The room had fallen completely silent. My coworkers blinked in shock. We were all stunned and likely in agreement that Sam had just lost his mind. I couldn't speak. Anger flooded my throat. *This has to be my karma for all the prior jobs I was bad at,* I thought, trying to find reasoning in this completely unreasonable situation. I could feel my entire body swelling with warmth. My ears were so stunned from what they'd just heard that it felt like church bells were ringing inside my head. Perhaps that was God chiming in trying to say, "Don't do it, girl. Don't go off."

Some weeks prior to this horrific exchange, I'd put in my letter of resignation. My first self-published book, *Words from a Wanderer,* was selling really well, and I thought I was ready to take the plunge into full-time entrepreneurship. There was so much I wanted to do that I couldn't with a full-time nine-to-five. My daughter was also set to start kindergarten, and I didn't want to miss anything. Despite my readiness to leave, when I gave my notice, Sam had begged me to stay. He even offered me a raise and showered me with praise about the fantastic job I was doing. "You leaving us would be a great loss," he had said, sitting across from me in the conference room. "We want you to grow here, and I think you can. Tell me how we can help you do that."

Against my better judgment, I had decided to stay when he offered me a raise. Perhaps change wasn't meant to happen quite yet. Maybe I needed to slow down, save more money, and prepare a better plan. *Was I rushing?* I often asked myself. And if so, *what was my hurry?* Truthfully, I wasn't rushing, I was just scared. Terrified I was going to crash and burn and look stupid for trying to do what I loved. Worried that I was going to be broke and struggling, which I couldn't afford to be. *What if I failed? What if my mom was right, and this dream I had was selfish and impractical?*

Now here we were, several weeks later. Hearing that I was low budget and essentially just a placeholder for receiving packages blew my mind. Self-doubt had kept me in the position longer than I should've stayed, but the incident with Sam was the one I needed. It's like the universe was telling me, *I tried to give you an out, but you didn't trust me. Will you listen now? Will this ridiculously hurtful encounter serve as your cue to get the hell out of there?* It did. It was time to go.

I placed the art supplies down, got up from the group, and followed Sam into the hallway. He turned to verbally lash out at me again. I stopped him midsentence and firmly said, "I don't know what's going on with you, but I quit."

"You what?" he snapped, turning so red that I could almost see the steam coming off of his skin. There was nothing more to say; he heard me. I walked back to my desk, "where I belonged," and started to pack my things. Sam emerged in the hall a few minutes later and calmly asked if I was sure that I wanted to do this, that things had clearly gotten out of hand. I looked up and said, "I am more than sure."

"Well," he huffed, "I will be deactivating your SmarTrip metro card effective immediately."

"Okay, Sam," I said, grabbing my belongings and walking out the front door. At the same time, UPS arrived with a boatload of packages.

"He'll get those," I told our delivery person, motioning to Sam.

Walking out the door, I felt liberated. I was choosing myself and refusing to be belittled by someone who thought he had control over me. I was also finally giving myself permission to do what I loved for a living, even if I was a little frightened. It crossed my mind that I'd just made an awful mistake, but nothing could've been worse than staying in a toxic work environment where I wasn't valued. Standing on the street corner, I called Ryan, my now-husband, pissed off and ready to fight somebody. He calmed me down and reassured me that I was prepared for this shift. That I was made to be exceptional and it was my time to rise up. I listened, tried to relax my nerves, and agreed. That pep talk was exactly what I needed. The next person I called was my mom. She worked a block away from where I was standing. I replayed the story for her, expecting that she would tell me to march my ass back inside and get my job back, but she didn't. To my surprise, she told me how brave it was for me to not stand for mistreatment and that she was glad I made the choice to leave. My jaw dropped. Change was clearly on the horizon.

The next day, it felt good to get up and not go build someone else's dream. Even though I would miss my coworkers, I didn't regret my decision to leave. I rolled out of bed, got my daughter ready for school, and started writing my second self-published book, *Love in My Language*. I was still selling jewelry at the time to keep money coming in, but that soon got phased out. I wanted to nurture writing with my full attention. This big life shift was my chance to prove to myself that I was shedding my comfort zone and ready for new beginnings to take root. I'd saved enough money living with my parents to prepare to move out without fear of becoming a starving artist, at least for the time being. I felt stable and excited for what was to come. I was ready to do whatever it took to unfold deeper into my joy and career.

Two months after quitting my job, I got an email from Ohio State University. They wanted to book me for a speaking engagement and pay me more money than I'd ever gotten in a single paycheck. When I got that email, I cried happy tears. That was the kickoff to my career as an author, facilitator, and speaker. I cried because I knew that even in my moments of uncertainty, there was someone out there who connected with my work and words. It had been a long time coming, through all the mistakes and job changes. There was plenty of fear and uncertainty during each ebb and flow, but I decided when I quit my job that I would fly or fail. I've been soaring and evolving since the day I walked out of that office in 2013. And while I am happily where I want to be in my life and career at this moment, there's always more work to be done. There's also more to learn.

I understand that every storm that passes through

is clearing the path for something bigger, brighter, and more bountiful.

There are so many different ways to honor my process.

I am leaning into the slow practice of mending.

There's no reason to rush getting it "right."

How do you want to change?
Think about things in your life that
need to shift and require your full
attention to do so. Make a list in your
journal of the changes you'd like
to make as you continue to evolve
into your best self.

# Self-Love

Disliking who I was came easily to me as a child. I wore self-aversion like a second skin, and I mastered the unhealthy habit of picking my entire existence apart without hesitation. As an adult, unpacking my past, upbringing, and childhood has brought a lot of emotions to the surface, some that I am still not ready to look in the face and confront. Navigating how I heal and move through trauma is a daily practice. And though I may not be willing to open certain boxes packed with pain, I understand that in order to make space for healing, all things must be rooted in love, and not fear.

Growing up, I never felt loved. At least not in the traditional sense. And definitely not how I saw some of my peers being loved, particularly by their parents. I often wondered why I was here. What was my purpose? Who needs me, anyway? And why would God, if there was one, give me *this* life? My sense of belonging, or lack thereof, molded me in an extremely unhealthy way. Unlearning self-hatred came with a unique set of challenges. This included removing the learned behavior of self-loathing and unhappiness, and replacing it with the possibility of self-love, fulfillment, and joy without relying on the validation of others. Without needing outsiders to love me first.

As a kid, feelings of rejection swallowed me like a rushing river—deep, cold, and turbulent. My earliest memory shaped my sense of belonging, not only in my family but also in my body. I was about seven. My mother and I were driving in her paint-chipped white Mazda. The seats were bland and stained. My eyes wandered as we backed out of the parking spot in a dimly lit garage. I was on her nerves; that seemed to be my resting place. More times than not, I could read *Why did I have this child?* written on her face like a journal entry. I remember feeling the fervor of her disgust and frustration. I must've done something that she didn't like. Walked too slow, maybe? Talked back or something. Who knows. But when she got mad, she got really mad. Her irritation filled the car with white noise and regret. Fearful and intimidated, I inched closer and closer to the passenger door, as if moving away from her might protect me from her wrath. In the thick silence, through clenched teeth, she looked at me and said, "Keep scooting and I'll push your fucking ass out of this car." At that moment, I felt what is was like to be dressed in hatred and disdain. Thoughts of inadequacy and confusion ran rampant through my mind like a stampede of wild animals running from their own shadow. That experience buried itself deep into my bones like marrow and stayed there as if I was born to carry it. I felt like I wanted to die. Because maybe if I died, my mom would find a way to love me.

Being so young, I didn't have the awareness to think that something could be wrong with her. That perhaps depression had swallowed Mom whole and wouldn't let her come back up for air. Or maybe she didn't love herself, and she was trying to figure out how to love me in the throes of that uncertainty but couldn't. I don't know what's worse; not being able to breathe and parent, or not being able to love and parent. As a mother myself now, I understand that the things we grapple with in the thick of remorse and redemption can try to define us, ruin us, and mold us, for better or for worse.

Looking back on that day in the car,
I can see how lacking self-love and self-
forgiveness crucially impacts how we show
up for others, including our children. I didn't
come from love or longing, and nurture
didn't live in our home. I felt trapped in
my own body from childhood on, scared to
make a move because the wrong one could
ruin everything. I was constantly longing for
somebody, anybody, to love me, see me, and
want me. In a sense, I was anchored by the
sins of my parents. Self-hatred sank its claws
into me and, at one point, wouldn't let me
go. I had to figure out how to love myself
by myself, and that didn't happen until my
midtwenties.

As I matured, the lesson slowly started to
present itself. When I turned twenty-three, it
became clear that I was not born a hostage
and I did not have to succumb to my circumstances. One day, something just clicked. I
wanted to take control of my life and stop
feeling like a victim. I had gotten tired of
hearing myself complain about what wasn't.
So I chose to focus on what was, face it
head-on, and do my best to fix what I could.
Not feeling loved or cared for as a child did
not give me the right to move through the

world carrying self-destruction on my back. That'd always been my excuse to act in ways that were meant to cause avalanches in my life. Realizing that certain things in life are a choice, I made the decision to free myself and find myself in the reflection of my own eyes and not those of whom I was trying to force to see me. It took me years upon years to intentionally shift my narrative and step out of the victim role. How long could I blame my upbringing and self-worth deficit on everyone else? My past couldn't keep speaking for my present. Trauma or not, I had to make the effort to rise from the ashes and soar. Nothing around me was changing to my benefit because I was not making space for it to. The older I got, the more clear it became that I was the common denominator in my suffering, so I needed to adjust. Self-love feels like looking yourself in the eye, taking a deep breath, and saying: I see you.

I deserve to see myself in the same
warm glow that I see others.

My light is abundant.

My joy is important.

I deserve to take up space.

Loving yourself isn't always
a beautiful process.

It's hard.

It can break you open.

It can wear you down.

Self-love is birthed in the
trenches of our darkest moments—
that's why the light feels so good
when we finally find it.

I have the strength to
touch where it hurts. I will
tell my pain that it's safe to heal.

In the throes of healing,
I may break open time and time
again to learn that the things
I thought I healed from still
need nurturing.

Explore your first memory of loving
yourself or struggling with how to.
Who taught you what you know?
What do you need to learn or unlearn?
Unfold the layers of your story and find
the root of your self-love process.

# Soothing the Suffering

I feel most at home in the silence of the morning. Opening my eyes to the rising sun finding its way, leaving trails of honey gold and hues of ochre and persimmon behind, blows my mind every time I witness the sunrise. It reminds me that all can be well and beautiful in life after the hush of the night's darkness.

But there are some days, no matter how stunning the sky is, when gratitude can feel like a distant afterthought. One morning, many years into my self-healing work, I woke up from an unrestful sleep. Things felt heavy and out of place. My off mood felt like a cloak, covering me and smothering my joy. I immediately felt like I wasn't going to be able to have a good day. And there weren't enough affirmations in the world for me to change my mind. It was going to be one of those emotionally hard days. What rocked me even more was the tough time I was having trying to figure out and shake off what was the matter. I hate not knowing what is wrong with me. I felt alone and worried and ashamed for feeling both of those things.

I called a friend, a spiritual teacher and life coach, to see if I was losing my mind. She told me to identify my grief triggers, because it sounded like something was coming to the surface that I normally might ignore. I rolled my eyes. "Grief triggers?" I replied with an edge in my voice. That is not what I wanted to hear at all. But in the same breath, I was filled with dread. It all came rushing back to me at once. The night before, I'd been having feelings of not being enough that stemmed from childhood. I'd been trying to figure out why I was even alive. What was my purpose on this earth? And wishing things were better and different for me. My inner child was having a tantrum: She wanted attention, and love. And those feelings had manifested in my heavy mood.

I'd worked so hard to identify ill feelings stemming from my childhood and hush them so they wouldn't be a distraction in my present-day life. I thought I'd put those issues to rest. So to have them rush back into my memory and take over my entire day made me doubt everything I thought I knew about the work I was doing on myself. Everything I thought I'd healed from. In my mind, I had arrived already; I'd done the work it took to address things that triggered me. And I was frustrated that I was second-guessing what I knew to be true about myself.

"Why can't there be a destination in this self-healing work? Why does it have to be an ongoing process?" I asked my friend. I told her I was longing for an end point. Trying to figure this stuff out, over and over again, made me feel like time was being wasted. Like I was stuck in some sort of endless cycle. "I can't change what I can't change," I said, "and that's okay with me. But I'm frustrated, and angry, that what hurt me then still seems to hurt me now." She let me go on and on before telling me, in the kindest way possible, to shut up and stop complaining. She reminded me that I knew how this process worked, so why was I dwelling on the pain of what couldn't be changed? My truth was my truth, and sometimes it exposed itself in messy and confusing ways, but that didn't mean I wasn't enough or worthy, she insisted. It meant I was still learning from whatever I thought I had already learned.

There was the lesson, period. I needed to accept that, until the end of my days, I'd never be able to silence my suffering, all I could do was try to soothe the suffering. My friend encouraged me to have a conversation with my younger self. To write her letters and notes when she started to emerge from the depths of my mind, begging me to remember her. As much as I didn't want to do that, I realized that it couldn't hurt to try—especially if it would help soothe me.

I started with the question, *What would I tell my younger self about mending after being broken?* The words of wisdom I would share with her would be rooted in vulnerability, softness, and strength. I'd tell her this:

*Hold your hurt, rest in your pain more often, stop running from fear. Don't be afraid to touch and face what scares you the most. Asking for help doesn't make you weak. Collapse into vulnerability; that is where you will find resilience. Take care of the soft and tender spots of your grief and process and bandage them up slowly. Rushing to rebuild won't make you heal any faster.*

I would tell her that it's fine to be a mess. It's good, even. An immense amount of magic can be found in the chaotic moments we encounter. The true process of mending has exposed itself in the thick of the moments that have shattered me.

After that eye-opening conversation with my friend, navigating the waters of suffering has been an ongoing quest for me. As days morph into years, I grow more comfortable with the fact that emotional hardship does not have an end point. Triggers will present themselves, and sometimes I don't know what the hell I am doing. But I take comfort in knowing that I have the ability to learn new ways to self-soothe when grief strikes.

That morning when I woke up feeling outside of myself, I forgot that I could find my peace of mind. That I had the tools to self-soothe. And that, too, is a piece to the puzzle of healing. Hurt and heartache will never be comfortable, but I have grown to trust that things can get better. I am also leaning into understanding that maybe, sometimes, things won't get better. And I'll have to keep addressing them and learning from them. There's an interesting lesson in that duality. No matter which way things go, I will continue to move forward.

Suffering has been an extraordinary and underappreciated teacher in my life. It's taught me how to heal, give myself grace in intense moments of grief, and recognize the importance of gently moving through experiences that cause tension, discomfort, and uncertainty. No one demonstrated how to relieve the inevitable agony that life would hand me. No one told me that I was in charge of it, either. I was left to figure out how to not only acknowledge but also understand the role I may have played in causing it.

Uncertainty with how to address my pain left me in limbo. Being where I am today, on the other side of some of my most painful experiences, is proof that we have the power to mend ourselves. Even in distress, and turmoil, I can heal the damaged parts of myself by releasing attachments to things I cannot change and letting go of the notion that I have to figure out my sorrow. The joy in my suffering has been standing in the truth that I can shift my story as I evolve and align more deeply with my possibilities, even when they seem far away. Giving myself unapologetic permission to look my heartache in the face and say, *You won't silence me*, has changed how I navigate pain. It's helped me nurture my inner child and it's transformed how I mother not only my children, but also myself.

We are taught to embrace the comforts of life, to stay in our lane, and play it safe. But that isn't reality. Something, no matter our contentment, will eventually remind us that life, healing, and learning how to take care of our emotions isn't a linear process. It's rocky terrain and will take us up and down many mountains as we discover our way. My friend reminded me that I made a commitment to not be silenced by my suffering, because it isn't sustainable.

Since that day, I have crawled into the mantra *Hurt happens, but so does healing.* Admitting that things aren't always going to be fine allows me to revel in the moments that are. The sunrises of my life deserve to be embraced, even on the days I feel blinded by the other stuff going on around me. Life doesn't stop when we grieve. Learning to soothe our suffering—choosing how to move through our pain—that is where the prize is.

The taste of undoing is
bitter and delicate.

Savor it.

Sweetness is coming.

My heart will stay soft
and filled with love despite
the hurt I will face. I am a student.

I am learning to allow my pain
to teach me, not harden me.

Think about the ways you can soothe your suffering. Experiencing pain and loss in life is inevitable, but having the tools to comfort ourselves through adversity and sadness can shape the ways we show up for ourselves and others. Consider how self-soothing can play a role in your healing process.

# Time

I see my eight-year-old self sitting at the bay window of the house I lived in with my mom. The front door was red with a brass mail slot that squeaked when it was fed. To me, it always looked like a mouth ready to gobble up anything, including my little arm that I would stick through it every so often. Bushes with leaves that looked like mini trees grew on both sides of the entryway and bore red berries that fell from their homes, littering the mulch below. I would sit in the nook at the window and wait for my biological father to come pick me up for a random visit. And in that waiting, I would count the steps outside leading to our door and watch the clock, wishing that time would speed up. More often than not, my dad wouldn't show. The sun would set as tears formed in my eyes. Through that repetitive disappointment, I developed a habit of wanting to rush through everything—waiting was too painful. But I was ignoring the lessons that time was trying to teach me: Life won't be what we wish it to be; no amount of wishing and waiting will change that. And that when we truly care, we make time for who and what we value. When I lean back into my past and comfort my inner child, I make sure to nurture that truth.

Time has become one of my greatest teachers. It's been a healer. A comfort to the sore spots that I've come to know and accept on my journey. With every voyage through vulnerability and every mountain of courage climbed, time has shown up, rescued me, and taught me how to be wiser, more tolerant, and more forgiving. I am learning how to loosen my grip, open my hands, and let the hopes of the past escape my palms. Time is continuously guiding me to a glory-filled life that once felt untouchable. I'm unearthing what it takes to be my best self every single day.

Time has done an exceptional job of teaching me how to care about myself. I've figured out how to invest my time in healthy relationships, a fulfilling career, and the legacy I want to leave behind. It's taught me acceptance and understanding and how to gather myself after being cracked into a million pieces with no "fix it" manual. I've become a work of art through times of neglect, uncertainty, and failure. Time has made it clear that being my own worst enemy was my truest challenge. Holding on to what could've been doesn't change what was, and expecting anything different to manifest from things I cannot change only creates a dent in the power I am attempting to stand in.

The greatest lesson I've adopted from time well spent—and time wasted—is that I am the gardener of my destiny. Digging dirt and sifting soil. Planting seeds and watching them grow, slowly and with an unrushed ease. With time, my harvest continues to produce, feeding me in new ways so that I can share my lessons of defeat and abundance with others. Time has taken me by the hand and revealed how to be okay with not being okay. How to stop pretending and performing for the sake of being seen and heard. I am not on a stage. And being anyone but myself would be a disservice to my purpose. I wore a cloak for so long. I felt like a fraud and I was running away from my authentic self. I was hoping that I could be what other people wanted and expected, all while slowly killing myself inside for not being faithful to my authentic path.

What I've been exploring more earnestly
is undoing and unlearning certain parts of
my story. And in that exploration, time has
been my greatest ally. I've been working
on letting go of the need to fix what feels
shattered and, instead, allowing time and its
even-tempered hand to do the work that I've
often pushed back on. No matter how ocean-
deep the pain has been, time has never
failed to offer clarity, perspective, and a
sense of peace.

I sometimes envision sitting next to my
younger self, near that bay window, in the
house with the red door and brass mail slot,
and holding her. Telling her that she doesn't
have to sit around and wait for anyone. That
time is too precious to waste counting steps
that no one is walking down. I picture myself
wrapping her in a hug, wiping her tears,
mothering her, and letting her sadness run
down my body like a river. I would remind
her of how special she is and how her worth
isn't tied up in how her parents could or
couldn't love her, and how she will be more
than fine. That her life will be happy and
filled with purpose, passion, and people
whom she won't have to wait on. I would
hope that she hears me with trust and curiosity, even through her dismay.

As a kid, I never imagined being an adult. I wanted to be grown but had no clue what it took. Retrospectively, I have no clue why I wanted to grow up so fast. It was likely because I felt that was the only way I would break through my independence and joy. When I became a mother at eighteen, adulthood still seemed like a mythical creature. Aging didn't seem real, yet time spread its wings and flew right above me, waiting to land. It was circling me like a hawk, waiting for me to realize that it wasn't slowing down for me. Now, fear of not having enough time eats at my soul. And I wake up some days longing for a pause button so I can make the most of my time on earth with the ones I love. Time isn't stopping or slowing down, and how we invest and spend it is almost an art form. I think about how it has shown me the importance of letting things be what they will and the peace that comes with relinquishing control.

As time marches on through each unfolding season, I realize that my story is just beginning. Every stormy day is a reminder to be patient and work for change while I wait for it to arrive. Time gives me the space to forgive with a big and open heart and to love deeply. I don't want to leave this world with

a bitter taste on my tongue, despite many
of my moments not being sweet. This journey isn't just about savoring the sweetness,
but learning how to swallow when things
become too much to bear.

To think back and know that I almost didn't
make it here blows my mind. I was a sad
girl, a lost girl, a misguided girl, who had
to choose between life and death. I went
from wanting to hang myself to choosing
to help myself. I went from being silenced
to screaming my truth from the rooftops
without feeling humiliated. I went from
being not enough to more than enough. I
learned so much about preparing for what
comes after the rain through surrendering.
Resisting kept me small. Grudges hushed my
voice. Pain held me captive and made the
little girl in me weep from wishing my life
was different. But despite the shifts, changes,
and challenges, I decided that honoring
who I am and where I've been deserves
to be celebrated.

Time has given me the space to outgrow
my old self; it's shown me how to release
so that expanding can be a part of my story
and life's work. I spent years being resentful
about what I didn't have, what I didn't get,

and how I wasn't seen or heard. I'm starting to understand that I can be angry without letting that anger stunt my growth. I can tell the little girl in me to go play now, that it's safe and okay, and she, too, can let go. That she doesn't have to sit in the window and wait anymore, and that her healing won't be steady, but her joy, if she chooses to bask in it, can't be compromised. Time has proven that I can be gentle with myself as I mend and become whole. I am being patient and giving myself permission to start over as many times as I need to.

There will be moments when I have to start from scratch and begin again—even after I've done intense work to mend.

There's always more to learn in healing.

My healing isn't linear.

It blooms and wilts as my seasons
in life change.

Starting over allows me to give myself grace, as I wade through the ebbs and flows of grief.

I am brave enough to
see myself, even when others
don't.

Choosing myself requires bravery and trust, even when I'm not chosen by outsiders.

I still believe in my worth and choose to rise up.

Rejection teaches me to uplift my spirit and redirect my energy, even when it's a challenge.

You don't have to know what you're doing to succeed, but you do have to be willing to try.

I am working through my mess.

I am sorting out my life.

I am finding peace in the midst of madness.

I am deserving of emotionally clean spaces.

Letting go is teaching me that I am not lacking, but receiving. I am acquiring knowledge, resilience, and room in my heart for something greater.

I am gaining perspective from what is able to stay and finding wisdom in what has to go.

Letting go isn't synonymous with missing out.

I have the power to make room in my life for shifting and joy. I am releasing what no longer serves a purpose in my journey with grace—

I will create space for change.

I am grateful to those who didn't love me enough to stay;

their absence taught me that self-love is my superpower.

What is time mending in your life?
How is it teaching you to be
transparent, patient, and graceful?

# Validation

The stories of others lived in my bones for years. Even before I became a mother, I felt like a home, an overcrowded one. Heavy, at capacity, trying to fit the stories of others in my body. I felt fragmented by all the stories I held. So I searched for people who could fit my pieces together, like I was some sort of puzzle or mosaic art. I was on a quest for togetherness and acceptance. *Somebody, anybody, see me, love me, please.* There was no such thing as feeling complete and enough. My need for validation was rooted in my belief that I was born a broken girl. I didn't know how to fix myself or find magic in the mess I was making, and I believed that in order to become whole, I needed someone else to put my pieces together.

I learned self-validation along my journey, but not without failure and backtracking. Lessons are built through trial and error. As I crumbled time and time again, it became increasingly clear that a person who needs fixing can't mend anyone, themselves included. Sharing myself when I was in pieces only led to more disarray, particularly on the dating front. I remember looking in the mirror at twenty-two, after my last failed situationship, and thinking, *When have you ever been good enough and intact, for yourself?* The answer was *never*. I was always counting on someone else to do that for me.

When I was twenty-two, I became fast friends with Richmond, Virginia. More often than I should have, I would hop in my car and drive several hours to see someone I was barely dating there. With the benefit of hindsight, I now see that we were really only in the business of having unexceptional sex, eating below-average food, and sometimes engaging in dull conversations about life, none of which were better than mediocre. None of which made me feel the thing I was looking to feel. I doubt he even knew my last name. Nevertheless, he was nice enough and handsome enough, and I was searching to find all those missing parts of myself that I wouldn't grow to know until years later. So I settled, and put a lot of miles on my car, driving from my home to his with this burning desire that he would want me a little more the next visit. He never did.

When I first laid eyes on him, I was smitten. We were introduced by his cousin, someone who would grow to be one of my closest friends. The three of us gathered at a sticky wooden table in a modest restaurant on a sun-filled day. The light confidently danced through the large bay window behind us, almost like it was celebrating something great about to happen. I was attracted to his warm, honey-brown eyes. They matched his skin perfectly. At first glance, his face looked monochromatic in the most beautiful way. I remember his smile doing its best to outshine the sun. As the hair on my skin raised with curiosity, I felt right then that he was going to be a problem for me, one that I wanted to solve and conquer.

In our short time together, I learned he was a poet and a rapper and a man who saw the black woman as queen. He was different to me. I liked that. No one had ever called me "queen" before, or maybe he made me forget anyone who had. Before he could even ask me my name, I fell in love with a cloud of foolish possibility. We were young and I was hunting for the love I refused to see in myself. I was on the prowl for a project. I wanted to be seen and wanted and loved. And he was nice enough.

Richmond became a place I looked forward to going. I enjoyed exploring the
small college town with its eclectic vintage
stores, vibrant museums, and rich history.
Hipster cool-kid vibes wafted through the
VCU streets. He showed me around, took
me hiking, and would occasionally hold my
hand. When he spoke, I clung to his words
despite him not saying much.

There were months of blurry boundaries
and an unclear relationship status. Lots of
pressured "So what are we?" conversations.
Me wanting more, him being more than fine
not wanting much. I remember climbing
rocks with him on a hike one day and thinking that he was the most cultured man I'd
ever met. It's funny how longing can create
fairy tales in our head. Atop the rock, water
rushed behind us, humming a melody of
strength and softness. Something shifted that
day. He kissed me, in a way he hadn't before.
Somehow we both knew our time together
was coming to an end. He pulled me close
and kissed me hard, like he was trying to
make something out of nothing. The water
from a nearby river rushed by, crashing
into rocks and fallen branches. Our kiss was
clumsy and awkward. I kept my eyes open,
looking at the forested area around us. I

may have even rolled them, realizing, finally, that I wanted the entire thing to be over, the drives to Richmond, the lackluster conversations, the stringing along. He just wasn't my person, and I wasn't his. Despite his charming way and sweet demeanor, it was crystal clear that he did not want me to be his girl. In that moment of clarity, I noticed that his eyes were closed. I could feel his breath graze my cheek softly. His hands were rummaging around my waist like he was looking for something he'd lost. It was evident that he wanted it to be over, too.

In that instant, I knew that even with his honey-hued eyes and kind smile that out-shined the sun, *nice enough* wasn't good enough for me. The way our lips touched, the lack of desire, and the realization that I was doing that thing again made every-thing else glow with clarity. I was reliving old patterns that I was accustomed to and comfortable in. The familiarity stopped me in my tracks. I was doing what I did best: giv-ing up on myself and my needs to settle and shrink into the heart and life of someone with whom I had little chemistry on a good day. I wanted more, even if I didn't have the language to voice it. I wasn't looking for another fling, and he, fairly enough, wasn't looking for a wife. What I discovered from my short-lived romance was that I needed to find out who I was and what I truly wanted, from myself and others. Shrinking to fit in wasn't working anymore. Swallowing the desires and stories of other people had gotten old and unsettling.

It's easy to accept the bare minimum when it becomes the narrative of our personal story. I was so busy searching for someone to make me whole that I lost the ability to build trust in not only my voice, but also my individuality. Richmond showed me that being alone is better than sharing space with someone who wasn't a match. I walked away with a clearer understanding that I had to stop settling and forcing and being okay with the scraps of people's effort and time.

Years later, I continue to learn that I can flourish and be complete with or without someone standing next to me. I am my own validation, which now feels empowering rather than isolating and unnerving. While life is not meant to be done alone, it's important to make room and hold space for intimate moments that don't require company and praise to press forward. Validation starting with me gave me permission to trust myself in new ways, while holding myself accountable. It is no one else's job to make me feel whole and good—only I can do that.

I am learning how to make meditation
out of the mundane. Washing
the dishes, walking to the mailbox,
or even slicing a peach can teach me
something. I will no longer miss
these moments, because I am leaning
deeper into paying attention.

What does validation look like in your life? Is it external or internal? Close your eyes, and take a moment to find a new way to validate yourself and your purpose.

# Love

The dense LA air was like molasses as I stepped through the Los Angeles International Airport's doors to the arrival area. The humidity tenaciously clung to my body as it if were my second skin. The strap of my cotton dress kept slipping down my shoulder as I tried to find my ride. He told me to look for his red Chevy Blazer, and I spotted him double-parked nearby. He saw me and got out of the car with a big grin on his face. I remember my heart starting to beat like it was going to slingshot through my chest. The hair on my body raised with excitement and nervousness. His tall frame and handsome face stood out among the crowd of people also trying to find their rides. He made my world pause for a moment.

We'd made it to each other, and I could not believe it. After six months of phone calls and FaceTime dates, Ryan and I were finally face-to-face and skin-to-skin. It was late July in 2014, a week or so before my twenty-fourth birthday. His locks were long and his big smile took over his whole face. *He is perfect*, I remember thinking to myself. And his memory was apparently very sharp because I was greeted with a fistful of sunflowers, my favorite, and a kiss, like we'd been in love all this time. The ease of comfort made me hyperaware that I just might have found my person. His tight embrace made me feel like I'd finally found the missing piece to my puzzle. "Hi," he said calmly, looking me right in the eyes. "Hi," I replied, looking up at him, not wanting our bodies to part. He grabbed my luggage and opened the passenger door to his '96 Blazer. My heart fluttered. *Oh, and he's a gentleman!* I thought. Every moment of that day felt unreal. Ryan said that he knew I was going to be his wife the second he saw me walk through the doors of LAX.

Ryan and I first connected on Twitter and we met at a good time in my life. I'd done a lot of self-work, and I was at a point in my journey where I didn't mind something serious if it happened, but wasn't looking. A year prior, I'd stopped having sex, stopped dating and entertaining people who I knew were temporary, and decided that settling was not an option in my life. Essentially, I stopped wasting my time and started figuring out who I was outside of motherhood and men. I wasn't happy with how things were going, and I wanted to feel fulfilled. The only person who could shift how things were going was me. So I pivoted and stepped into choosing joy for myself. Ryan caught me at a good time and in a good space.

Both of us seemed to be in awe of each other as we drove from LAX and hopped on the 405. We were finally together, sharing a moment in the flesh. Being with him felt effortless; it made sense. What we had wasn't fairy-tale romantic, despite seeming that way. Instead, things felt unedited and authentic. We were both a little anxious, but even then I felt like Ryan was an old friend of mine and we were catching up after a long time apart. Our first stop together was a little hole-in-the-wall diner that neither of us enjoyed. I was a vegetarian at the time and picked the absolute wrong spot for lunch. Ryan had fries; I had vegan chili. Both were underwhelming.

After our lackluster lunch filled with blushing cheeks and exchanges of *I can't believe you're here* looks back and forth, he took me to my friend Tonya's to drop off my things. My trip to LA wasn't completely centered around Ryan. Tonya was a close friend of mine, and I was in LA to celebrate her birthday. Ryan living just fifteen minutes from her was a plus and maybe even fate. I think I stayed with Tonya for just two nights, before deciding I wanted to be with Ryan the entire trip. Tonya was thrilled for me, for us, and for what was to come.

In the years leading up to that, I'd dated so many of the wrong people. "Dated" might be an overstatement. I had a baby with someone I barely knew and struggled to find my footing as a young single parent. At a point in time, a lot of my love life was rooted in low self-esteem, searching for belonging in the wrong places, and trying to find self-love in the hearts of others. Tonya had been around to witness quite a few of my setbacks, especially on the dating front. So to have her in my corner with beaming support gave me a bit of reassurance. I remember her meeting Ryan and saying, as we walked up the red carpeted stairs to her apartment, "Girl, I think he might be the one! I can tell, I've got a feeling." I shrugged it off and decided that time would tell and I wasn't going to put pressure on anything being more than it was, but that didn't stop me from smiling the biggest smile inside.

The connection between me and Ryan was fresh and exciting. I'd never come across a man like him before. He was calm, funny, and laid-back, but not in an obnoxious way. I liked that he was nice to me, and not because he wanted something but because his heart is too big to be anything but kind. Still, I wanted to keep whatever we were starting lighthearted. We lived 3,500 miles away from one another. There was no telling what would happen and I wasn't interested in getting my hopes up. I wanted to enjoy every moment I could by being present. That was a task, for sure. A big part of me was tempted to do the whole checklist thing with him. *Does he have this, that, and, oh yeah, that? Do I want to marry him? Would he be a good dad?* Pushing those thoughts to the side was a challenge, but I knew that this time, I had to let things be what they were without my added rumination.

Ryan had been in Los Angeles for three years but had barely seen any of it before my visit. Discovering what Southern California had to offer made our time together even more special. My first night in town, we stopped at the Griffith Observatory and watched the glowing city from above. The sun was setting and the sky turned intoxicatingly hot pink

and lilac. I remember him being nervous.
I remember reaching to hold his hand and
his palms being sweaty. I remember thinking
I could do love with him, but not wanting
to jump the gun. Taking my time was
extremely important. We'd built a long-
distance friendship and I wanted to keep
things cool, grounded, and rooted in that. I'd
never gotten to know any man long enough
to consider him a friend. Cherishing the
attention and affection that we were sharing
made me want to know him better than anyone else. We authentically cared about one
another and I think neither of us wanted to
mess anything up.

Over the next few days, we explored the
city. We saw our first movie together and
went to the Fairfax flea market, where Tonya
snapped our first photo together. My visit
to California would prove to be the pivotal
beginning of our love. I started to think
Tonya may have been right. Perhaps Ryan
was the one. I ended up extending my trip
because it felt wrong to leave. I knew I had
to get back to my routine and responsibilities
at home, but it was clear that I was falling in
love. In real love, not the kind I dreamed of.
I always imagined perfection and bliss, but
in the most unrealistic way possible. Kind

of like a Disney movie romance where the prince comes in and saves the day. But for the first time ever, I didn't feel like I wanted to be saved by love. I didn't want to fix Ryan, either. I wanted to enjoy him and let things grow and be lighthearted. What we had felt genuine, lively, and imperfect. We could be ourselves with one another with no expectations or worries. I could feel the love he had for me, deep inside my bones.

When my trip came to an end, I was prepared to go back to Maryland and see where things would lead. We had such a good time, and I thought things would only get better, but I figured we'd keep things casual. Ryan had other plans. A few hours before my flight, in the most unromantic way possible, he asked me to be his girlfriend.

He looked at me and said, "I don't want no other chicks. So what's up?" I cracked up laughing and returned his sentiments, "Well, I don't want no other dudes. So what's up with you?" In reality, I was shocked, because when we first connected he made it crystal clear that he was not a relationship kind of guy. It was pretty hysterical to us both that his mind changed, but I'm glad it did. We both agreed to try our hand at a long-distance relationship. Neither of us had really done this before. Being in a committed relationship felt foreign and a little strange. Before we met, Ryan was a true bachelor uninterested in commitment. And I was constantly failing at finding a nice guy. But for some reason, we both knew we were extremely sure about each other. Sure enough to give it a shot and see what could happen.

I'm convinced the laughter we shared and the fun we had over that first week gave us the confidence to be together. There was no pressure and we weren't trying to impress each other, we just were who we were— sometimes hysterically so. One morning, we were laying in bed and I had to pass gas. I was too lazy to excuse myself and go to the bathroom, plus I figured it would be small, silent, and undeadly. But instead, I let out the biggest fart in the entire world. "Whoa!" Ryan said wide-eyed. I played it off without missing a beat, "Relax, it was just overnight air." We both laughed so hard that our eyes were watering. I wasn't embarrassed and he wasn't grossed out. When we were joking about it later, he said, "I'm glad you got that out of the way quick. I don't have time for you to be hurting yourself because you're holding in farts trying to be cute." If it were anyone else, I would've likely ran out of there screaming in horror and dying inside from humiliation, but it was fine and funny and something we still hysterically laugh about to this day. He'll often say, "I knew for sure, for sure, at that moment that you'd be my wife. No questions about it!"

Ryan is the first man to make me feel like I could be my entire self with no filter. I didn't have to wake up pretty, my hair didn't need to look perfect, and my eyebrows being done or legs being shaved didn't give him pause one way or another. He made me feel seen and appreciated. His ability to listen, even when he wasn't a fan of what I was saying, blew my mind. Ryan was the first man to help me figure out what I was looking for in a partner just by being himself, and by accepting me in all my grit and glory without second thought.

After that first trip, I started visiting LA every six weeks or so to see Ryan. I would leave my life in Maryland and hop on a five-hour flight to Los Angeles. Ryan lived with his sister and her husband, and eventually I started to feel like I was a part of their family, eating spaghetti or insanely delicious potato balls from Porto's Bakery at their round kitchen table. Our long-distance love made each visit precious, and we sweetly savored every moment together, splitting our time between the beach, shaved ice and waffle spots, and museums with the most stunning views. We even did yoga together. My fondest memories with Ryan often center around food and finding the best hole-in-the-wall restaurants. We discovered new ways to have fun each time I came to town.

As amazing as things were going, being apart was laborious and a true test of patience and understanding. Being long distance took a lot of work and commitment, but looking back, it was beyond good for us. We learned how to communicate and keep in touch emotionally. When we weren't together, we made time for one another despite the 3,500 miles and three-hour time difference. Even when there were days when nurturing our love felt too difficult to manage, we stayed the course because of our belief in one another. I had moments of defeat and wanting to give up, especially when there was conflict in the air, but he wouldn't let me walk away. He had grown to know my fears and patterns, and instead of being impatient with me, he loved me harder. Ryan taught me how to relax and relinquish control. We would either work or we wouldn't, and that precariousness made me extremely uncomfortable, but like rapper Nipsey Hussle said to his wife, Lauren, you don't possess people, you experience them. Looking at love from that angle is something that took us years to learn through trial and error.

The biggest lesson that our long-distance love taught me was that I needed to learn how to trust someone who wasn't nearby. Immaturely, I thought being close by made a world of difference, but it didn't. Trust is trust, near or far. I had to learn how to go with the flow and not let the hauntings of my past dictate how I moved through this new relationship. That was the hardest part for me: letting go and letting love lead without fear of being hurt at every turn. Even through the self-work I'd done, trusting people, specifically men, was still rocky. The biggest risk I took with Ryan was not only believing that I could trust him to hold my heart but also trusting myself enough to let him.

Eventually, after about a year, and many discussions later, Ryan decided to quit his job and move to Maryland to join me and my daughter. We'd done a lot of evolving during our long-distance relationship and we were ready to take the plunge and dive deeper into the life we said we wanted to build. That step sealed our first chapter, and we began a new chapter together as a family.

Opening myself to Ryan and choosing to stand in love with him was a true test of my progress in self-love. There were many years where I'd convinced myself that love didn't love me and that I would be alone. I didn't feel worthy of love because, deep down, loving my entire self felt like a task I couldn't quite complete. I had people in my life candidly tell me that women with children were a single man's worst nightmare, and that no man would want to raise another man's kid. I had many moments of defeat because I assumed that those folks were right. When I took a year off from dating, sex, and settling, I started looking into what my life without a partner would mean for me. And it felt okay, because I had started the process of falling madly and deeply in love with myself, a practice that took a lot of time and energy. I know that the work I did on myself opened me to the experience of falling deeply in love with the right person and gave me the tools to make that relationship work.

Love requires vulnerability. For me, it continues to be a heart-opening experience that constantly shifts how I see the world and myself. Giving myself permission to stretch, soften, and let things grow organically reminds me that I can change and make space for joy in ways that I had never imagined. Meeting Ryan proved that love was not evading me and didn't have to be this foreign thing that only some lucky people got. Believing that I was more than deserving of love opened up a new way of life for me. Even when times are challenging in love and marriage, I don't doubt that doing life with Ryan is the right choice. Over our more than six years together, we've gained so much wisdom on how to live life as both a unit and as individuals. I'm glad I believed in myself enough to stop settling and start creating the life and love I desired. I'm proud that I let go, trusted the process, and let love win.

You are deserving of opening
your heart and letting love in.

Don't let the hurt of your past
or the doubts of others deter you
from building the life you long for.

I am capable of paving a new way for myself.

I will do the work.

Even in uncertainty, I can be great.

Think about what your love would taste like if it were a flavor. What would you like it to teach you on your journey toward it?

# Becoming

I remember wanting so badly to be a mother again. But the right way, this time. Not at eighteen. Not knocked up by someone I barely knew. And not in the throes of trying to find validation and love in empty places. Giving my daughter a family meant more to me than I can begin to explain. I felt I owed it to her, and to myself. We were worthy of togetherness, peace of mind, and joy. She deserved a consistent male figure in her life outside of my stepdad and a home with a bedroom outside of my parents' house. I remember wanting to become something bigger than myself, bigger than I was encouraged to be. My heart desired to live for a purpose larger than I could then imagine.

For the first five years of her life, I worked diligently to cultivate our own meaning of home. I did all that I could to get my life together so that I would be the best mother and woman I could be for us. I discovered the meaning of soul work during those years. I didn't realize that when she was born, I was reborn. I was a new human being. During that phase in my life, I sacrificed, I suffered, and I shifted. I lost friends, faith in my purpose, and the ability to live a full life along the way. I stumbled more times than I can count, over and over again. So much so that I learned to find joy on the way down. The climb to becoming was slow and at times unsteady, but well worth it now that I am on the other side.

Being a teen mother shaped me into the person I am today, even though the entire experience was wrapped in trauma, shame, and issues of rejection that went unaddressed and ignored. I am able to name that piece of my truth now. I own it all as a part of my story. Facing my healing head-on has been a point of contention and growth that I've learned to find gratitude in. Pieces from my past still sting, but I wouldn't have found my light without their undeniable presence. There were moments early on in motherhood when I thought I was doomed, cursed even. I had intense moments of guilt and constant worries that my choice to bring a new life into the world, under less-than-ideal circumstances, had set my child and me up for destruction and failure. I was terrified that I would face a tough time breaking the cycle of loss and longing.

No one taught me how to love or be loved. I didn't have anyone holding my hand and walking me through what nurturing looked like. Nevertheless, I was determined to fill in the blanks. Facing the fact that I was a statistic—young, black, and unwed—drove me to want more out of my life despite not knowing how to get there. That lack of awareness encouraged me to learn and do things differently. It encouraged me to do and be better than what I had experienced in life. The yearning for what I didn't have motivated me to become whole and full in ways that were once daunting and unfamiliar to me. For years, people looked at me with eyes of pity, and I looked at myself and felt humiliated. I allowed shame to engulf me. I was imprisoned emotionally, and the only way out was to stop playing the victim to my circumstances. I had to stop blaming outside sources for my sense of loss, lack of community, and misfortune. A large part of my self-work was taking accountability for my choices as an individual and understanding that I had the power to set the tone for my life. I had the resilience to be who I was working so hard to be for myself and my daughter. Rewriting my story and fine-tuning my narrative was up to me.

Building a sense of belonging became a priority in my journey through unfolding. On countless occasions, I was told that I would be and have nothing. That my life would be terrible and that my daughter and I would live in hardship. That no one would want to be a family with us because "Who wants a single mother, anyway?" It would have been easy to believe those lies and get distracted from the truth.

Becoming who I wanted to be, and not adhering to what negative and external voices were saying, taught me how to stand in my power. To lean into it, even without having the emotional support that I desired. I learned to support myself in the ways I thought others should. I was putting so much pressure on outside influences to bring me joy that I didn't realize my ability to be self-sustaining. That process wasn't easy. Despite feelings of loss and loneliness, it was essential for me to stand alone and figure out how I was going to get what I wanted in life.

Today, I take pride in my process. I trust my path. And I am proud of myself for becoming who I craved to be. The path to becoming was painfully tender, but I learned to trust myself enough to be someone I was told I wouldn't be. Moving through the process of change was a challenge. There were days when I knew I couldn't do it. It was too hard and big and scary to reroute. I felt engulfed by loneliness some days, like I was standing in shallow water alone calling out for help because I didn't know which way to swim. Independence was testing me; I could taste freedom at the tip of my tongue. Growth demanded all of my attention and more than just good intent. Meaning well and doing well are not synonymous. I was determined to prepare myself for the next chapter in my story. Giving my daughter the home, attention, affection, and life I didn't have was my driving force. Doing better and different from what I'd known for so long was my North Star, my reason for releasing and expanding.

Finding a partner to do life with was also something I dreamed of. I'd grown to understand that finding a partner required unyielding and self-sustaining love for myself. I was getting there. Being alone in the water was guiding me to dive deeper into my ability to show up fully for myself without the need to be carried by the love of someone else. I was taking on a new shape. As I did that, I wrote daily love notes to myself and poems to my future husband. I was insistent on manifesting my love into existence, not just through words but also action.

Eventually, I noticed things were starting to shift—my attitude, my outlook on life, my ambition, and my friend group, too. I spent a full twelve months being as introspective as I could. I found comfort in yoga, plant-based eating, meditation, abstinence, and holistic living. Things I never really thought I would be interested in brought me contentment and challenged me to explore who I was and who I wanted to be on a deeper level. Everything I once knew and took comfort in I chose to leave behind.

It was a lonely year, but becoming a new person had to start with the shedding of my former self. A reboot was happening. The sun was emerging. And it felt damn good. I found triumph in my new habits and practices. Making the radical decision to choose myself was a daunting and delightful task all at once. Deciding that I mattered and was worthy changed my life. I became a more patient mother, a kinder person, and a

woman ready to share her love abundantly.
I met my now-husband 3,500 miles away
fourteen months after I made the commitment to myself to stop settling and start
striving for greatness.

Transitions, big or small, are rarely straight-
forward. They require abandoning the parts
of ourselves that feel safe and familiar. It
is a massive task to intentionally choose
change over comfort. But it taught me to
trust myself more and embrace the shifts.
I've developed a new sense of gratitude for
the growing pains and heartache. The quiet
season in my life taught me to hold on. To
trust the flow of my river, even when no one
is around to help or guide me. Becoming my
true self was brutal, but the process brought
out the beauty in my life that I ached for. It
made room for more love and less judgment,
more self-belief and less fear.

I am capable of leaning into my resilience.

There will be people who can't see it,
but I will bloom to become despite who
stops to appreciate my growth.

Recall a moment when you started to notice that you were becoming your true self. What did it feel like and how has your becoming shaped you?

# Family

The roots in my life never felt firm. Growing up an only child, I often felt adrift, out of place, and unsettled. Since I can remember, I've always wanted to fit somewhere, but the world seemed to reject me at every turn. I never had the sense that I belonged to a family. Instead, I felt like I was just drifting, taking up space.

Over the past few years, I've been exploring what family means to me, and how the word *home* manifests in my life. There are many moments when I think about my biological family roots and feel brokenhearted, especially as I get older. I've grown to appreciate what and who I have, and in what capacity, but I still often feel a sense of loss. Describing my family dynamic is difficult to put into words. What seems to stand out the most is how detached everyone is, and how genuine love seems to be a wish upon a star. No family is perfect, but I've found myself longing for a sense of care, consistency, and community. Being in family spaces has never felt safe.

My husband's mother, Ileana, was the first person to show me what unconditional love could be. Her calls to check in or to wish me luck when something big or small was on the horizon, her meaningful embrace that felt like love itself, and her acceptance through adversity were new for me. Shocking, almost. Her presence was refreshing and unique. She made me feel like I mattered, which I wasn't accustomed to feeling in my own family. I remember her telling me to forgive my mother, because she, too, was a woman doing the best she could.

One Thanksgiving before we were married, Ryan took me home to Kansas City to meet his entire family. I was queasy with nervousness; I don't do well in big groups of people. I didn't know how to show up in such a large family setting. The pictures, the laughter, the hugs, and the outwardly expressed love terrified me. Being the new person in the mix did, too. The mental image of the entire encounter heightened my social anxiety before we even got to dinner. The minute we walked into the banquet hall of relatives,

I wanted to leave. My ears started ringing, my palms were itchy, and I felt out of place. The feeling of not belonging anywhere, of not having a family of my own that felt like home, washed over me. *Was I overdressed? Did my hair look okay? Will they like me and accept me?* Overthinking made my body feel empty and numb. The voice of self-doubt crept up my spine like a monster from under my bed. *Look at these people who love each other. You'd never fit in here; they're way too happy. You don't deserve this type of joy. You're trash. Ryan deserves better; why would he bring you home?*

I got up and went to the bathroom multiple times that night, just to escape the room for a few moments. I asked Ryan's sister-in-law when it was time to go just as many times. I was so overwhelmed and wrapped up in my thoughts that I wouldn't dare step out of myself to let loose, have fun, and quiet my distracting, negative self-talk. There were so many people—aunties, uncles, cousins, and babies—chattering and taking photos. Bellies were filled with laughter and good food. I felt completely adrift. In that moment of overload and fear, shutting down felt like my safest option.

More family came over to Ryan's mom's house later that evening. He was expecting me to come out and say hello, but I had no more energy. I didn't want to go say hi and give hugs or meet anyone new. I was in my own head despite how rude and self-absorbed that was, and I wasn't ready to climb out. The thought kept swirling in my head: *How do people do this?* It felt impossible for me to show up as even a portion of myself in such an unfamiliar space.

Eventually, all of our built-up tension resulted in a heated, loud, and intense fight—family in the other room and all. In the thick of our rage, I screamed, "I don't want to do this with you! I don't want a family." The room fell quiet, and I could see tears in his eyes. My words had cut like knives, a bad habit I picked up from my mother as a child. Verbal daggers were my go-to defense mechanism when I wanted to escape my fears rather than face them. Secretly, I hoped he would say, "Good, I don't want this either." I preferred rejection because it was easier than problem solving and admitting that I was flawed and vulnerable. I didn't feel worthy enough to be in his family. I knew what I was doing by trying to find a way out of the relationship. I was repeating what I'd so often done on plenty of occasions. I was running away from the unfamiliar and cowering back into my unhealthy space of comfort. In truth, I desperately wanted a family with Ryan. I wanted to marry him and have his children and grow old together, but I didn't know how. And staying meant I had to learn. The love I knew never stayed—it always felt conditional, and in turn, I felt like an outsider in Ryan's world, unworthy of being accepted and loved authentically.

Driving home from Thanksgiving dinner, I was drained. The car ride home was silent. I could hear the drumming sound of my heart beating violently. All I wanted to do was be by myself and recharge. Ryan was doing the thing where he tried to figure out what was wrong with me without asking, shooting me questioning glances, breathing hard while tapping the steering wheel, and parting his lips to speak but deciding not to. And I was doing the thing where I got unnaturally quiet. I could tell he was hurt by my behavior and confused about why I wasn't happy to be around his family. We hadn't mastered our healthy communication yet, so having hard talks wasn't an easy feat. My nerves were shot because I knew we needed to have a talk, a talk that I wanted to avoid. I had so much to say, but it was easier to just shut up so that I didn't make things worse.

My behavior that night was a *thing*. A big, bad, disappointing thing that Ryan's entire family noticed. I was embarrassed and doused in regret. And even still, Ileana loved me through that flaw. I remember expressing how I completely ruined everything, and she assured me that I didn't. She didn't judge me. Instead, she comforted me and made sure I knew that even in moments of disappointment, I was still family and still loved by her. And when I was ready to talk about what I was dealing with around my social anxiety, she listened with her whole heart and body and tried to understand. It was then that I realized I couldn't expect people to know how to show up for me if I wasn't willing to speak up for myself and name my needs. Ileana was one of the first people to make a soft landing space for me.

The admiration shared among Ryan's family in the banquet hall that Thanksgiving was so massive and genuine. It was something I'd never experienced before. Instead of acknowledging the beauty, it terrified me, and I didn't know what to do with it. I'd grown accustomed to not feeling supported, and I'd gotten used to shutting down in order to protect my heart. Despite the whirlwind of events that night, Ileana's relentless love and kindness encouraged me to step deeper into my vulnerabilities. Since then, I've intentionally made room for my voice in my relationships with my spouse and those around me.

What I miss most about Ileana is her softness. Her warm, contagious laugh, how she interacted with Ryan, the encouragement she gave us as a unit and as individuals, and the faith she had even in times of hopelessness. When she died, I wondered who would give me and Ryan what she did. Her love was rare and one of a kind. She taught me that family is sown through unwavering love, authentic connection, and intentional choices. Her legacy lives on fiercely. I see that clearly through her children and the people who loved her and knew her more intimately than I did. Ryan's mother is the reason I've clung relentlessly to the thought of building my own meaning of family.

Since her passing, Ryan has reminded me that we can create our own definition of community and family. I remember feeling certain of that for the first time when he said, "I'm not just your husband; we are family. Your close friends aren't just your friends; they are family." Each time I reflect on that conversation, it brings tears to my eyes. Many things in my life have been unspoken and carried away with the wind. So to remember that family and home are what we make them gives me a sense of ease and unity in moments of grief. It reassures me that I am not lacking, despite what my biological family looks like.

I have gained so much in my life along the way, and that Thanksgiving experience was a turning point for me. As I continue to walk through all that I walk through, I am working on having more compassion for my past and the people in it. I'm committed to finding my true self and leaning deeper into self-awareness while acknowledging my flaws. There have been plenty of moments where it feels smoother and safer not to address the things that break me down. But it has been in the breaking where I've discovered my belonging. Cultivating family has been a tender spot for me ever since I can remember. I've avoided many things because of the dynamics in which I was born. My greatest lesson has been facing what causes the most fear so that I can openly begin to heal. As I move deeper into my process of accepting and unfolding, I am striving to concede that there are many things I can't change in my life. Many things I wish I could. But my victory and joy can be found in cultivating what feels good within my own growing family, the family I thought I would never have.

I can make the hard choices
that I've been avoiding.

Those choices give me
the courage to become
who I say I want to be.

May you be brave enough
to choose yourself even
when others don't.

Healing is a soft
and slow process.

When you hear the word *family*, what comes to mind and how do you feel? Make a list in your journal of the joys and challenges you wrestle with when it comes to your familial relationships. Perhaps you've cultivated family in a nontraditional way. What does that look like?

# Learning to Breathe

I love Eastern redbud trees. When their dark branches are covered with deep lilac-purple flowers, I know that spring has emerged. The flowers remind me of botanical rock candy cascading from the sky or wind chimes waiting for permission to sing from a gust of wind. Their short-lived presence always sparks intense joy for me. Driving my eldest daughter to school one spring day, I excitedly pointed out the new purple flowers. She smiled and pointed to the daffodils blooming nearby, saying, "They look like little lions who eat the sun." We call spring the rebirth of beauty.

One recent spring morning, I ventured out for a rare walk alone to enjoy the emerging changes in nature. It had been raining for what seemed like months, and I needed to get out of the house. It was just after 7 a.m. on a Sunday and everyone was still sleeping. I filled my travel mug with coffee, slipped on some clothes, and descended the steps from our apartment. The whole building was hushed. Outside, the air was crisp. Light from the hiding sun played peekaboo, causing a chill that kissed my bare arms. *I should've worn a sweater*, I thought. The earth smelled of petrichor and sweetgrass, and it was a good morning to get up and move my body. Our neighborhood was quiet, almost eerily so. I almost felt like my slurps of coffee were going to wake the world up from its slumber.

I inhaled deeply for what felt like the first time in months, and was immediately struck by the fact that I was alive. Being intentional about my breath and staying present isn't something I am good at. I often forget to stop and be in the moment. There have been instances since being a mother of more than one child that I've longed to feel at home in my skin without grappling for tangible moments to cling to and remember. This particular walk reminded me of life's ease and small mercies. I was in tune and aligned. The silence was so amplified that noises around me sounded like they were in high definition. Grasshoppers, birds, rustling leaves, the swinging wooden fence of the flower garden nearby—everything had its own music.

As I walked, I listened and took deep breaths. In through my nose, 1, 2, 3, 4, 5, 6, 7, 8, 9, 10. Out through my nose, 10, 9, 8, 7, 6, 5, 4, 3, 2, 1. I was mindful of the rise and fall of my belly, the sensation swirling through my body, and the audible breeze following me. I was starting to feel at home, lighter, and more capable of "being here now" than I had been in months. It was almost as if before that lone morning, I was holding my breath. My stroll became a moving meditation, one step at a time filled with intention and appreciation. As I explored the neighborhood, I felt extremely privileged to be alive and in motion and in tune with the air circulating through my body. Perhaps that's the reminder I needed: to make time for myself and learn how to breathe again, unrushed and on purpose.

Discovering how to take care of myself has been a challenge. I still have moments where it feels forgotten. The women I knew and saw around were always taking care of other people, rarely themselves. Their faces and backs looked heavy with worry and concern for everyone but them, longing for relief and reprieve. Especially the mothers. I didn't want that to be me. I didn't want life to feel so heavy and laden with guilt for taking a second to breathe. I'm still learning the practice of harmonizing my time and prioritizing my needs. Society sends the message that women are to bend until broken and then find ways to get back up again while in pieces. Finding my breath during the hush of the morning encouraged me to stop overextending and start preserving some of myself for just me without guilt or shame or wondering whether it, or I, was worthy.

Being in silence can be intimidating. It requires my full attention, which is rare and cumbersome in my ever-evolving self-care practice. Getting still can be a burden on my plans. It makes me think and be in intimate company with myself, which can open a Pandora's box of things I've stashed away, like hurt I'm still holding and regrets that have gone unaddressed. But this is what I needed. To stop busying myself and hiding from uncomfortable thoughts. So instead of mentally sprinting through life, I stopped, slowed down, and expressed gratitude for all that was surrounding me. *You deserve this*, I said to myself. So as I continued to walk, I gave myself permission to be fully present with any and everything that came to the surface. Pleasant and unpleasant. And whenever I wanted to run, I decided to stand still and breathe.

I can lean deep into my existence by deciding to breathe and be in the present moment.

I am deserving of my time, company, and energy.

When is the last time you were in tune with your breath? Stop what you're doing and take five deep breaths, in through your nose, out through your nose. Feel the rise and fall of your belly. Extend gratitude for your life. Even if things aren't all good, be proud that you've made it this far.

# Healing

We'd been married for a little under a year when the news came knocking on my door. The message I read said things that cut me open and made me question what I thought I knew about my husband, our friendship, and the love we'd been tending to over the years. The sentence that stood out the most read, "I'm in love with your husband and I'm tired of crying over him."

Everything came crashing down. A single message shattered our ten months of marital bliss. And while the transgression happened before our wedding, it hurt and broke us down all the same. More than feeling betrayed, I felt sick, like I had eaten something that didn't sit well with me. I wanted to vomit. I wanted to leave. I wanted to cry, but the tears were too tangled up to dance down my face. I felt like I was drowning. Choked with confusion and chaos, I lost my breath and sat at the edge of the bed frantically trying to call it back home.

*What the entire hell is happening?* I thought. The words I was reading baffled me and stopped me in my tracks. I thought about playing it cool and not saying anything until I could get my thoughts together. Conversations never go well when emotions are high and swelling with indignation. I toyed with the idea of packing all his stuff up, leaving it outside, putting the latch on the door with a note that said, *It was nice knowing you*, and vanishing into thin air like we never happened. Like this didn't happen. But it did, and I couldn't hide from it, or run from it, or avoid facing the truth. So I called Ryan while he was at work.

"Who is Savannah*?" I asked.

Silence. Everything was quiet and numb.

"I got a message from someone named Savannah. Who is she?"

"I . . . I think I need to come home," he said nervously.

"Who the fuck is she, Ryan?"

"I'm coming home, please don't leave," he frantically replied.

I don't remember what was said after that. For a moment, I lost my mind. All I heard was static. My ears were hot and my vision was blurry. I hung up the phone, packed a bag, ushered my eight-year-old out of her room, and we left. Life as I knew it had changed. This heart-wrenching experience would change us, and our love, forever.

The following days were the hardest. We came home and Ryan left. We tried marriage counseling; it sucked. I was ready to call it quits. Life started to feel like a war zone. My ally had become my enemy. I'd worked tirelessly to become the woman I was. To love myself truly. To not take on other people's shit as my own. But this was different. Ryan wasn't just *other people*; he'd become my other half. I wasn't ready for this type of struggle.

There were moments so deeply rooted in pain and confusion that I thought my husband was my greatest adversary. Moving through this pain didn't seem possible even when I wanted it to be. The devil on my shoulder replayed my entire past and reminded me that I was indeed cursed—and I'd be stupid to stay and go to war for my marriage. The angel on my shoulder told me what I wanted: him. The suffering we both endured, the smudge left on our marriage, and the destruction to our trust ate at us both.

My whole life felt like a lie. Every bone in my body throbbed with grief. I barely recognized myself. Again and again I found myself wrestling with the same thought: *How do I love someone this intensely and not trust him with my heart in the same breath?* Fleeing felt easy and safe in my moments of uncertainty. Staying to repair what was broken felt threatening and way too vulnerable to stomach. Love didn't feel strong enough to fix the cracks in our foundation. Forgiveness felt foolish. I'd put a wall up, a barrier to protect my heart from any further devastation. But even that felt unsafe. I was resentful that we were here and hurting while life was still going on for everyone else. I selfishly wanted the world to stop so I could fix this first, and then carry on like normal. I yearned for a pause button, a redo, or something to lessen the blow. Nothing gave me solace. The healing process wasn't a journey I wanted to embark on. Things had been so good. We were settling in nicely as husband and wife. It felt like such a pain in the ass to unpack everything that had happened and look at it without turning away. No matter how far I wanted to run from my agony, there was no way it wouldn't come chasing after me.

Once the dust settled, and it was time to make a decision, I convinced myself that maybe this life partnership thing we had going was fictitious and unattainable. Perhaps it wasn't for us. We tried. Our apartment was right by the county courthouse. On many occasions I tried to muster up the courage to walk inside, without a care in the world, and file for divorce. All while blasting Lil' Kim's verse in "It's All About the Benjamins": "dressed in all black like *The Omen*." Like I didn't care about any of it.

But I cared every care in the universe and with every beat of my heart. So instead of walking through the doors of the courthouse, I sat by the trees outside that blossomed beautiful pink flowers in the spring. I counted the lines on the sidewalk and watched people flow in and out of the terracotta-colored building. I cried as I thought about Ryan's mother. On our wedding day she hugged me tight and said, "Thank you for loving my son. He's all yours now, girlfriend!" Her embrace that day was warmer than normal. Her energy was magnetic and hopeful. I tried my best to channel her spirit of faith, but it was tremendously difficult. I wished so badly that she was around for me to call. She was our rock. And her advice was more valuable than gold to us. I knew Ryan was somewhere wishing the same thing. I kept replaying her voice in my head. Whenever she heard us bickering, she would say, "Y'all better figure it out. C'mon now, get it together." That phrase became my mantra, for weeks and weeks. *Come on now. Get it together.*

In many ways it would've been easier to walk away, but I didn't want things to be easy. As unprepared as I was for this, I knew our relationship wasn't meant to be a walk in the park. Staying meant Ryan and I had to have gritty conversations that needed our full honesty and attention. We had to get rid of the blame and start focusing on unraveling the why and unearthing our how. *Why did this happen? Why wasn't it disclosed before we got married? Why didn't we feel safe enough with one another to speak up before the infidelity took place? How did we get here? How can we fix it? How can we rebuild trust in our friendship so that we don't find ourselves back here on either end?* All of these questions were painful and heavy, but we both agreed that if we wanted to mend our marriage, we had to start from the bottom and work our way up.

Forgiveness and healing didn't come overnight. It was rough for us for about a year. There were many moments when I wanted to walk away. Ryan was doing everything in his power to make things right, and at every turn I rejected him. I was hurting, and a part of me wanted him to know the feeling of devastation that I was wrestling with. For months I held him hostage to his mistake because I was so angry and hurt. But that wasn't helping us. That wasn't healthy for our end goal, and it wasn't the forgiveness I said I wanted to offer. Even though his actions were the reason behind my heartache, I eventually saw that I had to be accountable for my choice to stay and my choice to heal. Healing my heart had to begin with me if I wanted things to move forward. It wasn't up to my partner to fix me. His apologies and tears weren't glue that could put me back together. There was nothing he could say to give me comfort.

Letting go of what *was* and dedicating myself to what *is* created space for me to start over and love Ryan in a new and healthier way.

When we took a good look at ourselves and our relationship, there were cracks in the foundation that needed our attention. Everything else that would flourish after was a secondary result of fixing what was broken. The infidelity coming to light made us face each other in a way we never had before. Tending to such a painful wound required us to lean into one another, despite the pain. No more games, no more glossing over our conflicts. If we wanted our marriage to work, we had to commit to repairing ourselves individually to love one another authentically and radically. I think that's what his mother meant when she would tell us, "C'mon on and get it together." She wasn't talking about us as a unit. She was referring to our individuality. We chose to do life together, but that didn't exclude us from doing the hard self-work that partnership takes. Ryan and I assumed that having each other was enough, but it wasn't. We needed to get our personal inventory in order first before coming together as a unit. There were a lot of unresolved issues and heavy baggage that needed to be unpacked and released before we could start making things whole.

Realizing that it was time for me to move forward so that we could grow deeper in our love wasn't linear. Sometimes I would take three steps forward in my process and then thirty steps back. Healing for me meant getting myself together enough to learn from this big hurtful thing that had happened. In this experience, I learned that we don't own people. We can't stop anyone from hurting or disappointing us. And even those we love will make mistakes and let us down. No relationship is perfect and they aren't all worth repair, but finding the discernment to push through and gain insight from our experiences and connections can be where we find the depths of what we can withstand and overcome. After the dust settled and the wound started to feel less tender, I knew in my heart that Ryan and I could make it through this. We'd come too far to give up and walk away. We'd invested too much not to try. We would have to rebuild our foundation from the ground up. Our work together wasn't done: There was so much more that we wanted and needed from one another. Facing infidelity was the hardest thing we've ever gone through, but it's made us so much stronger than calling it quits ever would.

I am willing to release my expectations on healing and what it's supposed to look like so that I can make room for more self-compassion, self-healing, and self-love.

Reflect on what the hurt in your life taught you about resilience. Consider how you can take your healing process one step at a time.

# Identity

Tears poured down my face like an ocean. I can still taste the salt and feel the sting of the words: "You a little nigger baby, lil' nigga." And I can still hear the thick Puerto Rican accent and laughter of my elementary school friend Addy's stepdad as he addressed me. There was an awkward silence, my friend blinked, and her mom said nothing as I sobbed, my tears dripping into the stained tan carpet of their living room floor. Being eight years old, I wasn't even sure why I was crying, but I knew I felt attacked and hurt by the words directed at me. I had heard about the "*N* word," but I'd never been called it before. My little brain was stunned and completely uncertain how to process what had just happened. All I could do was cry and feel confused. The man made his way over to me and attempted to make amends by saying "*Nigger* is the word for black people." His breath smelled of beer, cigarettes, and sarcasm. I winced. Addy grabbed my hand in comfort. "You're black, ain't you?" He said.

"Be black and proud. Say it with me: I'm black and I'm proud." I said it, not knowing at that age that *nigger* and black pride were not even close to being the same thing.

"Now stop crying, lil' nigga." he concluded.

I don't remember seeing Addy again after that.

I've never forgotten that experience. It shaped me. It was the first time that I truly felt hated because of my skin color. I became hyperaware of my otherness from that point on. I would soon come to know that being black was more than a complex way to move through the world. My skin color, hair texture, and facial features all dictated how outsiders saw me and how I saw myself.

We didn't celebrate blackness much in my home, not like some of the other black children I knew. I remember going to Ina's house and her Caribbean parents cooking Jamaican food, speaking patois, and wearing clothes made from African fabric, their home smelling of incense. They kept tropical-looking plants around and covered their walls in beautiful works showcasing black art. It was new and forgeign to me, but normal for them. I liked it; I wanted something culturally that made me feel special, included, and celebrated. Looking back on those memories, I realize that my peers who had black pride also had traditions that were essential to curating feelings of belonging and identity. Back then it wasn't a second thought, but today I understand the importance of celebrating blackness as I raise and nurture my children.

That moment at Addy's house all those years ago subconsciously influenced me to make sure my children knew the importance of their diverse cultural identity as black people. My oldest daughter was encouraged at a young age to be proud of herself and all her differences. She is unique and beautiful, kind and smart. I was intentionally raising her to not only know who she is, but also to accept herself fully without second-guessing. So if someone had the audacity to call her a nigger, she would know not to take on their hatred as her own.

When she was in third grade, my daughter came home and said, "A boy on the bus told me my skin looked like the color of poop, and I don't understand why." As awful as it felt to hear the hurt in her voice, I replied calmly and wanted to do my best to use this instance as a teaching moment.

"I'm sorry to hear that happened today. Your skin is beautiful and brown. How did that make you feel?"

"It made me feel angry and upset! And I told him, 'No, it doesn't.'"

My heart felt at ease hearing her words. I was overwhelmed with relief and gratitude. Everything I had been teaching her manifested in how she handled her first taste of racism, on the school bus, in the third grade. Feelings were hurt, yes, but she clung to her truth despite it all. She displayed such cognizance and maturity for her age during a life-changing moment. It blew me away. She knew who she was. And she wasn't allowing anyone to rip away her sense of self.

"I am proud of you for speaking up for yourself. Sometimes people say hurtful things that can threaten our joy. But we always have to remember who we are in those moments. You did that so well!" I assured her.

That evening, I gave my daughter what my younger self needed: reassurance that blackness isn't a blemish or a burden and that her skin wasn't a curse or something to detest. It was important that she understood deep in her bones that other people's hatred or negative perceptions of us say more about them than about anyone else. I had her look into her bedroom mirror where I'd stuck sticky notes, each one with an affirmation to remind her of her truth. Together we repeated, "I am beautiful. I am black. I am smart. I am funny and kind. I am honest. I am magical. I am nice and vibrant. I am confident. I am inspiring. I am helpful and graceful. I am unbreakable and proud to be brown."

My greatest hope for that challenging experience in her life is that she felt less alone than I did at her age, and instead had a sense of feeling supported, heard, and held. The teaching moments I have with my children directly relate back to my childhood and what I was lacking. They're not only moments of learning for them, but they also offer the little girl in me the comfort she didn't have.

All that I am
inspires all that
I will be.

Who are you today and what gives you
a sense of belonging?

# Comparison

A few months after having my second daughter, I found myself packing and unpacking my emotional suitcase to see what needed to stay or go. I was making room for my new baby's joy and innocence in my life. Doing that meant shifting and moving things around so I could be my best self for her. As I unpacked my childhood in my mind, waves of grief washed over me. There was so much that I wanted, and felt I was missing, even as an adult finding my way. I found myself wishing someone had taught me how to mother these girls I was raising. Instead, I had to figure it out on my own.

Unlearning unhealthy patterns and habits is difficult, but relearning how to do things differently and for the better can feel like an even bigger task to tackle. As a new mother for the second time, my inner child felt trapped between wishing I had more love and nurturing growing up, and trying to accept what couldn't be changed. Days went by where my longing swayed in limbo.

How I was raised was a sore spot for me. I had grown up thinking that my experience was common. Unconditional adoration from parents was a foreign concept. There were always conditions. I didn't know I was grieving my upbringing until I saw other mothers and daughters interact once I was an adult. I remember a few years ago I went to visit a woman named Leah* whom I was becoming friendly with. She'd invited me over to her family's farm for lunch one summer day. The weather was perfect for July. Not too hot, cloudy skies, and a slight breeze. I was excited to get out of the house and into the sun. When I pulled up the winding gravel road, sheep were roaming behind a wooden fence on one side and horses on the other, grazing and moving slowly. Leah greeted me with a big smile and waving hand through the white screened porch door.

"Welcome!" she exclaimed as I got out of the car. "I am so happy you made it. Did you find the house okay?"

"I did! The ride was beautiful," I said, looking around in amazement. "Thanks for having me."

I had no clue that all this lush green land was only thirty minutes from where I lived. Driving through Leah's small town made me think of the life I sometimes dreamed of. Off the grid, in the middle of everywhere but nowhere, with land where my kids could play, catch lightning bugs, and laugh hysterically until their bodies were tired, a garden in the back, and maybe a chicken or two. I imagined me and Ryan sitting out on a large wraparound porch, drinking something cold while watching the sun go down, turning the sky hues of lavender and sea-salt pink. And in the same instance I caught myself thinking about how dark it must get with no street lights, and how inconvenient it must be to have to drive half an hour to get gas and groceries.

Walking in the front door, I took in the smell of freshly baked bread and honey butter. Leah's mother, Donna*, was in the kitchen preparing food with an apron tied around her waist. The countertops held ceramic plates adorned with sliced tomatoes decorated with edible flowers, garlic green beans, roasted shishito peppers, a perfectly roasted farm-to-table chicken, and a cheese plate with Brie and sharp Cheddar. A pleasant gust of wind danced through the open

windows, blowing the sheer off-white cur-
tains out of the way. It all felt completely
surreal—as if I'd walked through a portal
into another world.

I followed Leah through the kitchen to a
modest patio dining table accentuated with
wildflowers from their fifteen acres of land.
I was amazed. Donna joined us, and the
mother-daughter pair seemed to move in
tandem, their love shown in every motion
from passing the bread to pouring sweet tea
made with fresh ingredients from their yard.
Watching them felt like watching a movie.
I'd never seen this type of family dynamic
in my personal life. Their bond, their house,
their land—it all seemed too whimsical to
be true.

*Who really lives like this?* I caught myself
thinking. In the first memory I have of
sitting at a table eating, I was alone, with
my mother pacing the threshold of our
rented townhome's kitchen and dining
area. She was upset with me for drinking
all my juice before eating all the food on
my plate, snarling at me and demanding
I finish my spaghetti even though I was full.
She cursed at me and told me not to move
until I finished my food. "I don't give a shit

if you're full," she said. "You shouldn't have drank all that damn juice. Eat your fucking food and then take your ass to bed." I gagged as I tried to clean my plate while she watched, almost in amusement. She was the boss. I was the child. I vomited after being excused from the table, and then I was punished for wasting food.

Donna and Leah made me wonder what it would've been like if my mother and I had this type of closeness. Comparison started to set in, and I felt my body getting hot with jealousy. My self-pity was interrupted when Donna started asking me what I did for a living. I told her I was a writer, and she beamed with excitement.

"It's so nice to see you young people doing what you love for a living," she said in between bites of tomato. "Have you read *The Artist's Way*?" she asked with smiling eyes. "You've gotta read that if you haven't, seriously."

"I have. I mean, I am reading it. It's a book I pick up and put down often," I replied.

"Oh, darling. You've got to sit with it. You'll be forever changed. I remember reading it years ago, and my life hasn't been the same. Morning pages helped me evolve in more ways than one," Donna exclaimed.

I smiled. I hated doing morning pages—the portion of *The Artist's Way* that encourages a daily free-writing practice—but I was working on trying them again. We enjoyed each other's company while inhaling bread and butter. Our bellies were filled with the most delicious chicken and contagious laughter. We were enthralled with one another, listening to the stories that'd been tucked away in our memories. Most of my stories were about my children and my evolution from being a teen mom to a successful entrepreneur, wife, and mother of two. They both looked at me with a mixture of admiration and sympathy. I was used to my story leaving people filled with both joy and a twinge of pity.

Leah and her mom shared a lot of "Do you remember?" moments. As they went back and forth, I sat back and listened to their banter, dreaming of that type of motherly connection, and doing my best to find good memories from my childhood that might be lingering in a hidden place. In the same breath, I tried to remind myself that family dynamics aren't linear or simple. Surely Donna and Leah have their issues, qualms, and annoyances with one another, despite the pretty package. The truth was, in all of my comparison and feelings of lack and grief, I didn't know how long or hard they had worked to arrive at their closeness. Perhaps it's taken them years to form this bond and they're just now learning how to settle in and love one another in the ways they'd been asking for. But despite searching for common ground, I couldn't help but feel an immense sense of loss, and a huge difference between the love I was witnessing and the lack of love I had experienced.

After lunch we took a walk around the land. Leah was especially excited to show me the aging red cottage near the horse stables that served as their work studio, where they ran a small business together, dyeing fabric and making yarn, and again I was floored by a mother and daughter stepping into creative work together. I was certain that my mom and I would kill each other if we even thought about working together. It became clear to me that I was absolutely in a real-life fairy tale. As Leah opened the door, it creaked and light snuck through the wooden beams from the upstairs floor. Skeins of yarn dyed with turmeric, beets, and avocado pits were hanging from steel nails in a doorframe. They created the perfect hues of canary yellow, sepia, and pink quartz. Leah saw me admiring them.

"Those are the color swatches for this season's collection. My mom dyes them by hand," she shared as I grazed my hand against the perfectly twisted textiles.

"What's it like working so closely with your mom?" I asked.

Leah looked around to make sure Donna wasn't trailing too closely behind. "It's really freaking hard," she said with an exasperated chuckle. "I love her; she's great! Don't get me wrong. But she can be a lot. We are different in a lot of ways, but she means well." Leah continued, "I moved out here because I needed a change—the city was too busy and life was passing me by. Living at home with my parents is a beautiful challenge, but my life is slower now. A rooster wakes me up every day and we have fruit dropping from the trees out front that we can gather and sell at the local farmers' market. Most days I feel like I'm dreaming. The grass is greener here, for sure, even with the parental challenges." Then she turned to me and asked, "How about you and your mom, are y'all close?"

*Oh great*, I thought. *Now it's my turn.*

"We aren't not close," I said. "We've come a long way. Our relationship has changed since I became an adult. And there are definitely boundaries in place that make it easier for us to be in relationship with each other."

"Yeah?" Leah replied inquisitively.

"Yeah," I answered.

I wanted to talk more about what I meant but I knew it would ruin my day. There were so many conflicting feelings rising to the surface and I didn't want our nice time to be rained on by my sob story. But from the look in Leah's eyes, she seemed to understand exactly what I was saying.

Hearing Leah express a gentle and almost unspoken compromise that she has with her mom left me with feelings of compassion for my own mother. My mother wasn't the most doting or nurturing parent to me, but she's grown and softened to be a phenomenal grandmother to my children. Change is possible, no matter how it shows up. As much as I wrestle with what I didn't have, another friend reminded me to lean into what I do have. So I try to focus on the ways my mother did show up and support me when I needed her most, regardless of our perceived closeness or lack thereof. Focusing on the failures of our family dynamic, and carrying that with me as a grudge, wasn't helpful. It turned the boundaries I told Leah about into a barrier that felt impossible to push past. And as much as I want to be angry for what the little girl in me didn't get, it's unfair to punish people for their pasts. Especially when they are trying to show up in the present and prove that things are different. That they are different.

As I drove through the countryside, back to my side of town, I made a list in my head of how my mother has displayed love in her own way. In an effort to hold space for compassion and understanding, I decided against comparing that list to how I wanted her to show it. As trees passed me by for miles, I started to search for my first positive childhood memory. I was an only child and my mother worked a lot, so my nana played a huge role in taking care of me. Recalling my mom's affection, I realized it was often exhibited in the form of gift giving. When I spent weekends away from home at my nana's, I would sometimes come back to a bed covered in new clothes. One time, I opened my bedroom door and the denim outfit I'd wanted was neatly laid out on my bed. The jean jacket was embellished with an obnoxiously large silver glitter mustang horse on the back. On the left leg of the pants was a matching glitter horse taking up half of the midnight-blue denim. The outfit was horrendous by today's standards, but I was a thrilled ten-year-old ready to strut my stuff and leave a trail of glitter behind. My mother didn't hug me or make a fuss afterward. She simply said, "I'm glad you like it," and walked away.

There were no frills in her offerings. They merely were what they were. Giving me things was her way of showing that she cared. Regardless if I needed anything new or not, gifting was her display of hard work and attention. We may not have had many dinners together around the dining table or affectionate interactions, but we had a home that she worked hard to give me even under the immense pressures of life as a single black mother trying to make a better life for her child. Materially, I never wanted for anything. I had it all. I don't remember us struggling, even though she was raising me alone for years. There's something to be said about that.

And when I came home pregnant at seventeen, after my mother's initial rage and disappointment, instead of kicking me out, she and my stepdad helped me raise my daughter. We became our own version of a village. I was able to go to college, find my footing, and figure out my life. Without my mother's support, that would have been impossible. So while our relationship isn't a fairy tale on a farm, I've come to see that it's something that deserves less criticism and more praise.

Comparison is teaching me the importance of compassion. As I continue to unpack my emotional baggage and reflect on my childhood, I am learning to navigate each emotional entanglement with more grace for myself and those I'm in relationship with. My time with Leah and Donna opened up a new chapter in my story. When I left our lunch, I was carrying a new perspective and outlook on life. I realized that no relationship is without its challenges, even if it looks ideal from the outside. And I began to see that while it was easy to focus on my mom's deficiencies, if I reframed my perspective, there was also a lot to appreciate in her. Later in the week, my mom came by to watch the kids. Without asking, she folded all of our clothes and labeled the baby's items by size and season. There was no fuss, there were no hugs or frills. Before walking her out, I turned and said, "Thanks, Ma." She replied with a nod and a wave goodbye, "I'm glad I could help."

I am freeing myself of comparison
and making space for understanding,
empathy, and forgiveness.

I am a work in progress, and
I will continue to unravel
and make space for ease as
I learn my way and walk my path.

Think of a recent comparison you've
made in your life. Take another look
and consider how comparing can
teach you what you have, not what
you're lacking.

# Dedication

Sex had become a taxing, anxiety-provoking chore that neither my husband nor I could enjoy. What was meant to be filled with pleasure morphed into a planned endeavor that required a lot of prep work. Ovulation kits, check. Basal body thermometer, check. Ideal cervical mucus conditions, check. The best sex position for sperm to travel and reach the egg, check. Menstrual cup for holding sperm close to the uterus after the deed is done (I read that worked on an outdated online forum), check. Sex life becoming a chemistry project, check, check, and check.

We had been trying for almost two years to conceive with little to no luck. To be fair, before turning our sex life into a science fair, we got pregnant eleven months into deciding we wanted to grow our family. But shortly after finding out what seemed to be the news of a lifetime, I miscarried and we ended up back at square one. I'm still not sure what we mourned more, not having to try anymore or the pregnancy itself. Perhaps each was just as devastating as the other.

My husband and I were exhausted. We were young, too, as if that mattered like we'd thought. I was twenty-seven and Ryan was thirty. Surely vitamins and diet change would do the trick. But there weren't enough vitamins in the world to answer the question, *Why isn't this working for us?* I was convinced that I was being cursed for having my first child out of wedlock with someone I didn't love, back in 2007. Perhaps, even, the abortion I had was the reason God was punishing me. I didn't even believe in a God who harshly punished out of spite, mistakes, and bad judgment, but in my search for answers, there were so many questions and possibilities I wrestled with. On top of it all, my husband *did not* want to go to the doctor. Trying to bring up the notion that we needed a doctor's visit felt like a fight with a bull, every single time. My husband and all his optimism often keep me centered, but his "it will happen" and "let's keep trying" did not comfort me or give me hope in this instance.

I didn't want to solely rely on hope and prayers. I couldn't. We needed to pair hopefulness with help. There were many moments when we did not see eye to eye in our journey to a baby, and everything we wanted seemed beyond our reach. Trying to conceive was emotionally taxing. The twenty-four months and some change felt like decades. We lived in a foggy state of the unknown, fear, bad sex, sperm analysis after sperm analysis, and confusion. It was more than hard. And what burned the deepest was not being able to make the baby we so desperately wanted to shower with love and kisses and care. Our respective worlds started to feel small in their own unique and challenging ways as trying to make a baby took over our lives. I kept thinking, *What the hell is wrong with us?* At one point in time, I swore we were allergic to one another. I saw that diagnosis on a show once, *House* or something. It made sense for a split second, and then it didn't. Nothing ever made the sense we wanted it to make.

The only way to find answers was to go see a specialist, so we finally did. I need answers to problems, so I was ready: pen, paper, and imaginary lab coat, like I was on staff at Shady Grove Fertility. Ryan, on the other hand, was hesitant and far from thrilled, but he obliged. This was a scary and big thing for us. In retrospect, I can understand

Ryan's fear. We didn't want to get any earth-shattering news. Neither of us wanted something to be "wrong" with ourselves or with each other.

Many Google searches for gynecologist, urologist, and reproductive endocrinologist appointments later, we discovered the culprit. Mild male factor infertility. My husband's sperm was essentially categorized as low, slow, and abnormally shaped. We now like to think of them as laid-back and in no hurry, just like the human they belonged to. Our exceptionally great fertility team wasn't even sure how we got pregnant at all the first time. And they attributed the miscarriage to the challenged sperm. The good news was we had a treatable diagnosis. The bad news was that it was unlikely that we would get pregnant without some sort of intervention. Despite the route we had to take, we felt pretty good about our chances with an IUI (intrauterine insemination), a fertility treatment that involves placing sperm inside my uterus to increase the odds of fertilization. Surely, we thought, it wouldn't take as long as the science-project sex we were having. The process was less invasive and intense than IVF (in vitro fertilization), not to mention way more affordable.

So we tried it. Eight times. With no success. Eight more months of letdowns and negative pregnancy tests. Eight months of Ryan leaving semen samples for the fertility specialists. Eight months of having his sperm inserted through a catheter into my body. Eight months of my legs spread like the greater-than and less-than symbols, my vagina carefully propped open with a speculum like a door you don't want to close, and my feet resting oddly in the exam table's stirrups. After each insemination we wanted so badly for that try to be the one. During the fifteen minutes of "don't move until the timer goes off," we'd talk about our hopes and dreams and baby names. But each time we tried wasn't our "it" time. Our hearts were heavier than boulders for more than two hundred days as hopes faded into the depths of uncertainty. Our arms were empty carrying nothing but longing and defeat.

After our final IUI, the endocrinologist told us it was time to start thinking about alternatives. The cycles were not working. He was right. And we were wasting our money. It was hard to face that we needed more help than anticipated. We sat down with the doctor and looked at the numbers and statistics. We weighed the pros and cons and worries.

He drew us diagrams, too. All the information made me dizzy and agitated. The data said our chances of getting pregnant would double with IVF—manually combining the sperm and egg in a laboratory—using PICSI, a method of selecting the best possible sperm for fertilization before injection into the egg. Oh, and we were looking at spending around $27,500 from start to finish. Hearing that number made me sick, but a life without a child with Ryan made me sicker.

I'd reached a point where I was taking this infertility thing personally. I wanted to kick its ass. There was no way we would walk out of that fertility clinic without a womb full of a potential baby. This experience wasn't going to defeat or define us, even in our darkest moments. But as feisty and fired up as I was for us to come out on top, it was my turn to be hesitant and nervous about moving forward. Ryan was ready for option two. He'd had enough of the creepy recliner chairs (that he wouldn't sit in) in the sperm deposit room, unsatisfying *Playboy* magazines, and attempting to have perfect aim in a specimen cup. I don't blame him. But there was something about IVF that terrified me and made me feel like an alien. All the medicine, injections, and money spent gave me anxiety. We had the money in our savings, but what if it didn't work? What if I reacted adversely to all of the medicine? What if things went well, *but* our embryos got switched somehow at the lab, and I gave birth to someone else's baby? The worst-case scenario thoughts made me lose sleep. Why did we have to go through all of this? Why couldn't this be easy?

Despite being nervous, I agreed that moving forward with IVF was best. We got very lucky and had to pay only a tiny portion of the price tag for the IVF because our insurance covered the rest. I took that as a sign that maybe our rainbow after the storm was preparing to emerge. We did the shots, and Ryan became a pro at administering them. He dubbed himself a medical professional after the first go-around. My body reacted fine. I didn't bloat at all like some women do. My follicles—the sacs where immature eggs develop—were ripening up wonderfully like plump peaches in summer. And the retrieval of those twelve mature follicles went seamlessly. Ryan said I came out of the operating room sucking my thumb, which made us both belly laugh. Perhaps I was channeling our soon-to-be baby? Another telltale sign of hope, maybe.

Ryan provided one more semen sample and then we waited for the doctors to work their magic. One by one, in a petri dish, they would insert Ryan's perfectly selected sperm into what the doctors called "stunning" eggs for fertilization. And then we waited for science and spirit to do their thang. I envisioned the process like this: Sperm and egg meet, yet again, after a long game of cat and mouse. Sperm finally shows up correct and ready to impress egg with all his glory. They fall in love and inevitably, because conditions are unrealistically perfect, become embryos that look like hatching galaxies of oceans and stars combined. A true mixture of love and science and miracles.

The day our nurse called to give us the news, we were waiting by the phone for her sweet voice to spill the beans. "We have good news," she said. She told us that six of the twelve eggs fertilized perfectly. The embryos looked beautiful. Huge grins spread across our faces. Ryan had that look in his eye. I knew he had faith that we were closer than ever to what once felt eons away. The next few days seemed to drag by like honey dripping from a spoon as we waited to hear how our embryos developed before implantation day. Then the day before implantation, our nurse called again. I could feel the warmth of her grin through the phone. She told me they had a beautiful embryo. She said the doctor and embryologist were so pleased. All that was left was for me to come in and get my blood drawn. *It is happening*, I remember thinking. *This process is coming to an end, and it's going to work in our favor.* It was the first glimmer of hope I felt deep in my bones, hope that Ryan had all along.

The day of my blood draw our nurse called with the news that my levels were slightly higher than they wanted them to be. The doctor wanted to wait to do the implantation out of precaution of a failed IVF cycle. My heart sank to my feet and dread started to creep up my throat like lava in a volcano. My body turned hot. I started to sweat. *Everything was going so well; of course we'd hit a roadblock. Because we wouldn't be us if we didn't*, I thought. *Nothing is easy for us. We have to fight for everything.* I wasn't sad this time that things may not go our way; I was pissed and desperately wanted to throw a tantrum like a child. I was tired of sparring with infertility. We'd been knocked down plenty of times over the last twenty-four months, but we were not going down again. My anger turned into determination, and Ryan fueled my fire with support and "Hell nos" and "Wait for whats?" There was no way mustering up four more weeks of patience was an option for either of us.

I called the nurse. "I want to talk to the doctor," I said firmly. "We want to know our odds." The doctor saw us the same day. He explained our chances would be slightly lower because of my levels. He pulled out his charts and data and pens and papers. Ryan and I decided that we didn't care. We had had enough tightrope walking and losing and living in fear. Either it would work or it wouldn't, but we weren't going to not try, because then it definitely wouldn't work. Our doctor made it very clear that the embryo might not stick, but he knew we were ready to give it a shot, so he went through with the implantation.

To everyone's surprise, the embryo stuck. We finally got pregnant and stayed pregnant. Overjoyed would be an understatement, but I didn't take a sigh of relief. As elated as we were about the pregnancy, I was unexpectedly terrified. Loss and infertility had traumatized me. The first trimester was tough. There were moments in the beginning where I thought someone was playing a cruel joke on us. Days went by when it felt like we weren't *really* going to get to have the baby. That, perhaps, all of what we went through was in vain and for nothing. My hope and faith in my body wavered. Fears of miscarriage haunted me. I had vaginal bleeding and spotting on and off throughout the first ten weeks of pregnancy. I wore panty liners daily to monitor the bleeding, which only reminded me to not get too comfortable or too happy or too anything because this baby wasn't ours yet. The anxiety and fear of loss were always looking over my shoulder.

I didn't breathe easy until our beautiful nine-pound baby girl, Ila, was in our arms earthside, crying and ready for her first feed at my breast. Through it all, my husband was the safe haven I needed. When I filled with worry, he reminded me that we were built for this. That getting back up was in our blood. Loss taught us how to stick it out when we wanted to quit. It showed us the importance of partnership and patience, of being mad as hell at the universe and God and sometimes at each other, but still doing our best to love fiercely through the storm anyway. Looking back, we championed for what we wanted. We tried our damnedest not to give up. We fought so hard to stay in the ring.

Looking back on all we've endured, I feel a new sense of resilience. Walking through a miscarriage, countless disappointments, endless fertitility treatments, and emotional chaos demonstrated that we have so much to learn about ourselves, as a unit and individually. Despite the adversity we faced, we learned so much about our bodies and sexual health. After all we've gone through, I feel like a fertility specialist. When our daughter turned one, we decided we wanted to start the process of DNA testing our five remaining embryos and getting pregnant again. We were ready to get back in the ring.

But life had a different plan in store for us. Before we moved forward with getting our embryos tested, I found out I was pregnant. Naturally. Unplanned. Unexpected. We'd been told that our chances of natural conception was low and unlikely, but twenty months after Ila was born we welcomed another beautiful baby into our family. Dedication's greatest lesson was to prepare for the rainbows, because you never know when one will catch your eye and capture your heart. It taught me to fight hard for what I want. Because of this experience, I now believe the unimaginable is possible. There was no way Ryan and I could control any of this—the mess or the magic. We both had to learn the importance of relinquishing control and trusting the process despite the discomfort, uncertainty, and heartbreak. I am stronger than ever, and I feel confident in my ability to persevere and find resilience in trying times.

Change won't always feel good,
but it's a powerful teacher.

It teaches us to be resilient
and make room for abundance,
and it shows us how dedication
can help us grow in love and life.

Lean into loss and think about
what it continues to teach you.

LESSON 14:

# Acceptance

Gathering around my uncle's mahogany table to break bread and tell stories was a tradition for our family. Going to my uncle's house was special for everyone involved. Whether it was football games, holidays, birthday parties, or just because, hopping in the car and heading up the Beltway was something we all liked doing. My uncle and his wife had the most space, and all the kids had the most fun there. During the summer, the trampoline was a favorite, and in the winter, sitting around their firepit roasting marshmallows for s'mores sealed the deal. Being at their house was a treat, and they seemed to enjoy hosting. In fact, their home felt so open and warm that I even asked them if I could get married there. Ryan and I tied the knot on their deck in 2016. It was perfect.

I never imagined that things would so abruptly change out of nowhere just a few years later. But suddenly, everything was different. The last time we visited the house was for Thanksgiving in 2018. After that visit, my mom, grandmother, and I were shunned. No one knows why or what changed. Our family is small. It's essentially my mom and her husband, my nana, my uncle, his wife, and his kids, and me and my husband and kids. I'd been used to this dynamic for years. Not having a large or close family was a part of my story that I had grown to accept. This little family was all I had, and when it was time to gather, we did so without hesitation. I've tried to replay the night of Thanksgiving to scan the scene to see what could've happened to cause the shift. Maybe it was the conversation about race that my uncle's mother-in-law seemed to be perturbed by and uncomfortable with. "I don't see color" was the first thing to roll off her lips, as to be expected. Perhaps it was the story (that was supposed to be funny) about my uncle and his wife in Northern California being the only white people in an Asian part of town, when in fact my uncle isn't white like his wife, he's clearly black. No one laughed. Or maybe something happened after Ryan and I left that we weren't aware of. Nevertheless, as I mold and make my own family traditions, I've had to come to terms with redefining what it means to move through familial spaces. I'm learning how to honor people's silence even when it's being weaponized. And I'm becoming okay with simply not knowing or ever getting closure with why things are the way they are.

My grandmother sat across from me one Sunday and cried over the family rift. She was seventy years old, and it pained me to see her heart breaking in front of me. This is the woman who practically raised me, who took me on vacations when I was a child, who comforted me after brutal beatings at the hands of my mother, who spoke up for me when enough was enough, and who prayed for my safe return when I strayed. She was the strongest woman I'd known most of my life. Tears dripped from her cheeks as I hugged her, saying, "I'm sorry. I know this is hard for you." Her son's silence had gotten to her. She was confused and hurt. She wanted answers and to make things right, despite not knowing what went wrong, but instead was greeted with the hush of uncertainty. I had a lot to say, but didn't because it wasn't my battle to fight. I could have said that it didn't surprise me much that this was happening—this is our family's dynamic. Unhealthy communication, conditional love, and resorting to silence when difficult feelings are caught in the pits of bellies. Before I learned boundaries and self-accountability, I was the same way. And on my worst day, those unfavorable traits try to grab hold of me. Destruction always seems easier than the work of reassembling and acknowledging the very stories that break us down.

As she cried for our family, my nana and I sat and talked about things I'd never heard her say before. Like any woman who becomes a mother, she made mistakes along the way and in retrospect could've done things better. Her life as a single mother who gave birth at sixteen wasn't uncomplicated. I leaned in and listened.

Her story of rejection and feelings of failure were all too familiar. It felt like I was listening to a generational curse where doing the best you can is never quite good enough to break the cycle. Something I'm learning as I continue to embark on my journey and write my own story is that the trauma of my family runs deeps. We all have our shit. It takes profound introspection and personal hard work to dismantle suffering. Breaking the chains of unhealthy cycles begins with acceptance. Facing rejection is a challenge, but it continues to teach me how important it is to accept what I cannot change. I wanted my nana to see that. I wanted to tell her that other people's baggage isn't ours to carry, and when they hand it to us and walk away, we can choose to leave it where it was placed. But how do you tell a mother that her son's rejection has nothing to do with her and everything to do with him? As a person raising my own kids, I know that it's hard to fathom them growing up to be adults who may have qualms with how I raised them. And it's scary to think about not throwing their emotional belongings on my back and taking it with me everywhere I go.

Practicing acceptance shows me that the baggage of others, even adult children, isn't mine to bear. I came to that realization while healing my own wounds related to my childhood and how I was mothered. For years I wanted my mother to own her shortcomings the way I saw fit. I perhaps even wanted her to suffer for being a "bad parent." But what I grew to understand was that she did her part, and doing mine didn't require reparations for the past. The only way I could heal was to acknowledge, accept, and appreciate what is, not what was. Navigating things like difficult family ties, rejection, and the unspoken has enabled me to take full control of my life.

One of the greatest things I've gained from this experience is self-trust—trusting myself and my instincts even when I feel like something is being lost or left behind in the process. I've had to work through loss and unpack patterns of codependency, which feels all too common in my ancestry. As I listened to my nana talk, I realized how important it is to create more room in our minds for understanding what we can and can't control. We can't make people love us, see us, talk to us, or understand us. Being family doesn't always mean that those things are a given.

It was exceptionally difficult for me to come to that realization. Most of my life, I yearned for things to be different. As a child, I convinced myself that I had been kidnapped from a loving family. I often prayed that my rightful parents would come rescue me. Coming to terms that things were what they were devastated me for years. Acceptance isn't rooted in trying to force others to be cognizant of their actions, or demanding that they show up in ways they aren't capable of. It's the practice of doing our own personal work when it comes to being in relationships with people. While there may be a lingering longing for clarity as to why my uncle decided to separate himself, he doesn't owe anyone an explanation. The truth is, he may not even have one.

As painful as it's been, my uncle's distance has helped me further understand how I want to behave in relationships with people, family, and friends. His silence has taught me the importance of not blaming others for how I react, but instead learning to speak up during moments of discomfort or angst. It's shown me how I can be a better listener, mother, and wife. It makes me want healthy dialogue and clarity that's not covered in the cloak of speechlessness. Being silent doesn't solve conflict, problems, or hurt feelings. If anything, it can make things worse and harder to recover from. When silence is used as a power move to express resentment and disdain, or to oppress another, no one wins. I saw that clearly in my grandmother's tears.

Acceptance is teaching me to cultivate a table that doesn't run out of invitations for a seat when adversity strikes. No matter the issues that arise, I hope I am making a home for my children, and those who enter it, that allows love to live even after disagreements or misunderstandings. Leaning into what I cannot change means making intentional space for me to rip out the weeds of toxic cycles planted in the soil of trauma. Silence and rejection do nothing but distract from the main thing most of us yearn for: love, compassion, and community.

I will continue to expand from the things that threaten to dismantle my peace of mind.

I am doing my best to make space for acceptance and understanding, even when I am rejected.

What is acceptance trying to teach you?
How are you learning to accept what
you cannot change with compassion
and grace?

# Forgiveness
## (A Note to Self)

The pain from old wounds sometimes lingers, clings to you like a second skin that you can't seem to outgrow. Perhaps, even, makes you want to forget who you are and who you were and all it's taken to get here. But today, you are still standing. I am proud of you and your becoming. There's an air of self-awareness that you've grown to know deep in your bones. Where you've been and what you've walked through has shaped each footstep that you have left behind. And still, even though you've reached new heights in your quest and have come so far, there are some feelings of regret sprouting within the pieces of your story that you'd rather let slip away.

But that's not how pain or pursuit of understanding works. You can't pretend the aching doesn't exist. You can't silence it. Why would you want to? Where is the lesson in that? Instead, sit with it all. Breathe through it and remember to cry. Give it life and let it go. Perhaps what scares you the most is not having that lingering feeling of suffering waiting for you to drop the ball or turn that corner. Remember, the goal isn't to escape, become numb, or ignore what hurts or haunts. It's to acknowledge, accept, and appreciate all that comes with the ebb and flow of healing.

Transformation comes in waves. Deep down, you know that you're a work of art—abstract, filled with meaning and discovery. You've made time to mend what was broken and tend to what's been hurting. And still, forgiving yourself seems light-years away. You're worthy. You're allowed to let your guard down and become friends with forgiveness. You are braver than you think, softer than you know, and more resilient than you let yourself see. I am proud of you for trying every day like you do.

It's a challenge to create a new narrative when the old one feels like what you deserve. To forgive is to let go. To let go is to relinquish control and get acquainted with your vulnerability and courage. Opening your heart to the unknown is a challenge, but keep working on it. You are finding your way, despite the roadblocks that appear. That counts for something. You've made mistakes—some bigger than others, some more self-destructive than you'd like—but do not swallow your regret and let it simmer in the soul of your body or the pit of your belly. Forgive yourself, even for the things you hold with deep remorse. Give yourself permission to release shame. You are not who you used to be. You're more than your mistakes. Your past was practice, and everything you've walked through has helped get you to where you are today.

During your low moments, trust in the power of self-forgiveness and what it can teach you. Each shortcoming, stumble, trip, and fall has been a lesson. You will make more mistakes. Release self-judgment. Carry yourself in love even when it feels like too much to fathom. Forgiveness will always teach you something about where you've been and how much further you need to go. Self-forgiveness makes room for you to continuously discover the importance of holding space for compassion and clarity. You owe yourself the same tenderheartedness that you think others deserve. Trust your worth. Know it and own it. Even when the damage runs deep, I hope you take a moment to be gentle with yourself and your ever-evolving process. Before you can start forgiving others, you have to learn how to forgive yourself. Self-forgiveness is an act of community service. It takes practice, dedication, and the ability to lean in and be truthful with what stings.

Shrinking isn't an option anymore. It's time to show up and be big. Growing up, you carried a lot of self-destructive behavior on your back that caused you to sink and plummet. You held on to things that didn't belong to you. Being let down, having insecurities, and holding on to deep-rooted feelings of abandonment made seeing yourself, and your true potential, a challenge. But look at where you are right now. In this moment, you're still alive and breathing, even if it feels complicated and heavy. You don't have to carry your trauma so close to your chest anymore. Unpack it. Leave things behind and start over as many times as you need to.

Shedding doesn't happen overnight. You're unfurling and growing in new ways daily. Growth takes time and patience. Advocate for yourself. You are powerful and you have a say about what comes with you. No matter how strenuous life gets, keep trusting your ability to emerge like the sun after a storm. You'll always find your way home to yourself, even if you get lost along the way. Forgiveness teaches you time and time again that you cannot change what was, but you can always choose to give yourself grace and press forward into what is possible. Allow self-forgiveness to show you your potential and vigor.

Forgiveness is not a burden, but a blessing. Be flexible in your process. Give yourself permission to create a new path. Believe in your process. You will have to forgive yourself again one day for what you did or didn't do. Let that be okay. You won't always make the right choice or do the right thing, but your intention is pure. Trial and error creates space for fluidity and becoming your best self.

Make room for flaws, give them air to breathe. Stop hating yourself for failing and for not knowing. There's always a possibility that you won't know better the next time. You are a work in progress. Every piece of pain you've felt has prepared you for the moments in your healing where you have to show up fully. Be tolerant as you mend and take on new shapes. You are not broken. You are always whole, even when things feel like they're falling apart. And to those who have hurt you, splintered your heart, made you feel small, and rejected you—offer them mercy so that you can learn what true freedom feels like. Gripping on to grudges wastes time and energy. It will distract you from being your best self.

Start slow. There's no need to rush your process or gather your feelings all at once. One of the greatest gifts that life offers is the ability to understand that everything you encounter won't be what you want it to be. And even still, you can rise to the occasion with a soft, magnanimous heart. Forgive yourself for not knowing, not trusting, not caring, not understanding, and not getting back up when things felt too burdensome to hold. Forgive yourself for repeating the same thing and not learning from the past. Forgive yourself for the shame and guilt you carry. Forgive yourself for not finishing and having to start over. Forgive yourself for self-sabotaging and settling and thinking you were not good enough. Forgive yourself for not trusting your worth and deciding that selling yourself short was the only way to get by and be seen. Forgive yourself for staying too long when you should've left. Forgive yourself for not loving your body enough to value it as sacred. Forgive yourself for wasting time and being unkind and getting off track. You are worthy of everything good you thought you weren't.

Learn to care for yourself radically. Your small victories count, too. Your heart is big. You can do this. Some days will be tougher than others, but I am challenging you to find your strength embedded in the obstacles. You are valuable and deserve to be held in a space of lightness and empathy. Allow your pain to teach you that it never lasts as long as we think. You will continue to gather lessons as you move through conflict, relationships, love, loss, and finding what feels like home in your soul. Trust that you are in charge of every ounce of joy that fills your body.

You do not need outside validation to be happy, free, and authentic. Self-celebration is your birthright. Give yourself permission to be flawed. Give yourself space to self-correct and reroute. You are deserving of your own mercy. The sun will always emerge after the rain; you've just got to be committed enough to do the work while you wait it out. Love yourself through every hardship that presents itself. We are all doing the best we can with what we have.

I will remain grounded in my belonging
and will continue finding new ways
to be soft with myself.

I don't always have to be perfect
in my healing and unfolding.

My mistakes have made me more
malleable and open to learning
and understanding.

I am doing my best and trusting
my path without self-judgment.

Learning how to forgive is tricky. Sometimes, self-forgiveness is even harder than forgiving someone who has wronged you. Think about some ways you'd like to lean deeper into forgiveness and learn from the challenges that may come with it.

When I first started this journey of finding
out who I am, nothing made sense. I thought
I had to have everything figured out and
in order, but I didn't. My life felt like a box
filled with junk I didn't want, emotional
trauma that I thought I needed to hold on
to, and projections I took and tossed in
just because I thought that maybe some
were right and true. But in reality, I needed
to empty out that box and start over, taking with me only the things that I wanted,
owned, and used. Tools and lessons that
would serve me well on my journey. The
scariest thing about that was having no idea
what I wanted to keep and what I needed to
get rid of, and it was terrifying to be forced
to believe in myself enough to figure it out.
No one had ever asked me to think long and
hard about what I chose to carry with me or
leave behind.

The rainy season of my life lasted years
before I started to do the work that was

required of me to feel fulfilled and happy. I'm sharing this to say that if you're stuck in a rut right now, if you're looking for a way out, and if you're ready for things to be different, empty your box. Unpack and leave behind anything that is hindering you from being your best self. Running, hiding, and making excuses is always the easy way out. I did it for years. It got me nowhere. Transformation has to start with wanting something better and healthier. It's also one of the most uncomfortable things you'll face, but you are worth the chance.

I hope this body of work inspires you to start taking the steps toward diving deeper into your personal goals, lessons, and practice of becoming. If you're anything like I was, fear may be telling you not to try. But fear is also a distraction from finding joy. You have a purpose waiting to be uncovered, even if you can't see it in front of you. I went from believing my life was worthless to intention- ally finding meaning, even in the mundane things thrown my way. We were not born to stay the same or to be stagnant.

As far-fetched as it may sound, we were created for a reason. No matter our upbring- ing, lack of love, traumas, triggers, and everything else in between, there is something special nestled between who you are today and who you can be tomorrow. We are ever-changing beings, longing to be loved and cared for. But first, we've got to find ways to do that for ourselves. There are so many excuses that can be said about why we can't and won't change. In all honesty, those same excuses will stick with you and hold you back if you're not dedicated enough to trust yourself. Keep this close to your heart: You are in control of how you show up in the world. My hope for you is that you make the revolutionary decision to be big and not shrink for the comfort or satisfaction of others. Give yourself permission to bloom wildly without regret. Dance in your rain, scream, cry, shout, and remember who you are every single step of the way. As Maya Angelou once said, "Live as though life was created for you." Trust in the work you're doing to become who you've been trying to be. It won't be a walk in the park. The trek will likely be a shit show, but try anyway. Being knocked down isn't the green light to stay on the ground. You don't have to be an expert on life to be successful or well put together. Trying and failing and learning is where your growth and knowledge reside.

Even when things aren't going as you think they should, trust that you are made to be flexible. Don't be afraid to take on a new shape. Self-discovery is all about trial and error. It's an imperfect process that only gets better with time. Give yourself permission to be whole and enough on your own terms.

I'm not here to pretend that learning from pain is a joyful thing. It's not. It hurts like hell—sometimes even worse than the pain we've endured because we tend to carry it for so long, even if by mistake. The memories, the sensations, the sadness, and the life changes that come along with being devastated are etched in our bones like names in cement. But I can truthfully say that my brokenness taught me how and where to discover my softness and entirety. It has helped me become the person I am today. Being open minded and kind with myself as I moved through the things that broke me down was and is a radical act of self-care and perseverance.

The more we unfold into our healing, the more we can become whole. Commit to doing the work. Encourage yourself to show up—that is how you start.

My prayer for you is that you're brave enough to trust your process. So as you morph and encounter things that cause earthquakes in your life, as you face storms that you'd rather not walk through, and as you empty out your boxes to start over, know and believe that you are not broken; you are becoming. Heartwork is likely the hardest work you'll do. As you start to uncover and find new parts of yourself, things will begin to make more sense. Don't feel pressured or rushed to find your answers. Take your time and invest in your transformation. You owe yourself the opportunity to write a new narrative and stand tall in your truth as you press forward.

Be prepared to reroute and get lost along the way: There is no requirement to know where you're going or what you're doing. And a major lesson that I hold near and dear to my heart is that there is no arrival point when you're on a path of growth. You will learn something new and transformative every step of the way. I hope you believe in your ability to be bigger than you once expected. You are victorious in more ways than you know. It's never too late to prepare for triumph after the rain.

## ACKNOWLEDGMENTS

I extend my deepest gratitude to my husband, my
first and true believer. Thank you for not doubt-
ing my art. Thank you for letting me read you my
worst work and my best. Thank you for trusting
me to write about you. You are poetry embodied,
and the best chapter of my story. All ways, always.
To my firstborn daughter, Charleigh, a true talent
and teacher. I love you beyond the moon and
stars. You changed my life and inspired me to be
my best. I hope you run after your dreams and
lean deeply into your truth, forever and ever. To
my rainbow baby, Ila, I love your light and vibrant
soul. You made our family so much brighter
when you were born. Keep glowing, sweet girl. To
Maximus, my third daughter, you are the greatest
miracle. To Ileana Watson, your love changed me.
I am honored to have your memory embedded in
my heart. To my mother, Victoria, for keeping me
alive and being a phenomenal grandmother. We
are lucky to have you in our world. To my nana,
thank you for covering me in your prayers. To
my stepdad, James, thank you for being a kind,
generous man of few words and the best Pop-Pop

my kids could ask for. To my sisters-in-law, EJ and Sada, thank you for sharing motherhood with me and making time despite the distance. I am glad we are in this together.

To my sister-friends: Tonya, Ajolique, Josefina, Yasmine, Erika, Safa, Denisio, and Racheal. Thank you for being my chosen family. I couldn't imagine not having met you all—you've enhanced my life for the better.

To the people who've changed my life through their work, offerings, and truth: Jamila Reddy, Lisa Olivera, Niaje Wells-Hall, Jodi Westrom, Gianné Nascimento, Erica Chidi Cohen, Christine Platt, Angel Anderson, Morgan West, Farrah Skeiky, Sashee Chandran, Sophia Roe, Vanessa Cardenas, Vyana Novus-Magee, and Saran Toby. Thank you for making space for me, working with me, talking with me, and believing in my mission. I am grateful for your time, energy, wisdom, and generosity.

To my agent, Cindy, you are a force to be reckoned with. Thank you for believing in me and reminding me of my worth. I am so happy that I have a woman like you advocating for the work I do. You remind me that I am exactly where I need to be.

To my editor, Rachel, and the Chronicle Books team, I am honored to call Chronicle my publishing home. Thank you for trusting in my work and giving me space to create freely.

To my readers, new and old, thank you. Without your support, this author's life would be difficult to come by. I am grateful that you picked up this book. Words can't express how honored I am that my work has the chance to settle into your home and heart.

To my younger self, thank you for not giving up at life, even when it was hard not to. The world was better with you in it and I am glad you stayed through the rain. Despite feeling out of place most of your life, you found your way. Your hard work paid off. You taught yourself how to acknowledge your pain when it surfaced and spilled over. I am so very proud of the choices you made. Your ambition, courage, and brave heart paved the way for unrestricted blooming. Every drop of rain was worth it. I love you.

To the mentors in my head: Oprah Winfrey, Issa Rae, Brené Brown, Maya Angelou, bell hooks, Abigail Thomas, Julia Cameron, Nikki Giovanni, Audre Lorde, Toni Morrison, and Michelle Obama. You all are lighthouses of wisdom and encouragement in my life. Thank you for what you offer the world!

Ryan Spearman

**ALEXANDRA ELLE** is an author and a wellness consultant living in the Washington, DC, metro area with her husband and children. She became a writer after experiencing the healing benefits of writing through therapy and journaling. She teaches workshops and retreats throughout the world to help people find their voices through storytelling, poetry, and narrative writing rooted in truth without shame. Her mission is to share self-care practices and build community through literature and language.